Praise for
Everyday Happy Herbivore

"Lindsay gets it. She blends guidance, ingredients, and tradition with HEALTH! *Everyday Happy Herbivore* overflows with information and recipes from every corner of the globe, and they will fill every corner of your belly with plant-based goodness."
—Jane and Rip Esselstyn (author of the *New York Times* bestseller *Engine 2 Diet*)

"*Everyday Happy Herbivore* will ignite your love for cooking. The recipes are easy, quick to prepare, and delicious. Not only will Lindsay's low-fat vegan cooking help you stay slim and healthy, your taste buds will thank you many times over."
—Neal Barnard, M.D., president of Physicians Committee for Responsible Medicine

"*Everyday Happy Herbivore* is easy to use. We look forward to trying every one of the recipes. This is one rare cookbook where we do not have to make major alterations in ingredients (like leaving out the oil). We recommend it to followers of the McDougall Program without hesitation."
—John and Mary McDougall, bestselling authors and founders of the McDougall Program

"Lindsay is a vegan rock star. Another epic cookbook destined for greatness!"
—Mark Reinfeld, executive chef of Veganfusion.com and coauthor of *The 30-Minute Vegan*

Everyday Happy Herbivore

Over 175 Quick-and-Easy Fat-Free and Low-Fat Vegan Recipes

LINDSAY S. NIXON

BenBella Books, Inc.
Dallas, Texas

BenBella

BenBella Books, Inc.
10300 N. Central Expy, Ste 400
Dallas, TX 75231
www.benbellabooks.com
Send feedback to feedback@benbellabooks.com

Printed in the United States of America
10 9 8 7 6 5 4 3

Library of Congress Cataloging-in-Publication Data is available for this title.
978-1-936661-38-1

Copyediting by Shannon Kelly
Proofreading by Stacia Seaman and Iris Bass
Cover design by Kit Sweeney
Text design and composition by Kit Sweeney
Index by Lindsay S. Nixon
Printed by Bang Printing
Brody's Gluten-Free Flour Blend recipe (p. 303) courtesy of Katie Olson/Brody's Bakery
Photos on pages ix, 22, 23, 47, 189, 238, 240, 244, 249 and cover photo of Tortuga Rum Cake
    courtesy of Kimberly Roy, roboticwhimsy.com
Photo and recipe on page 17 courtesy of Angela Liddon
Cover and author photos by Jeremy Cox

Distributed by Perseus Distribution
(www.perseusdistribution.com)

To place orders through Perseus Distribution:
Tel: 800-343-4499
Fax: 800-351-5073
E-mail: orderentry@perseusbooks.com

Significant discounts for bulk sales are available.
Please contact Glenn Yeffeth at glenn@benbellabooks.com or (214) 750-3628.

Dedication

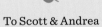

To Scott & Andrea

Table of Contents

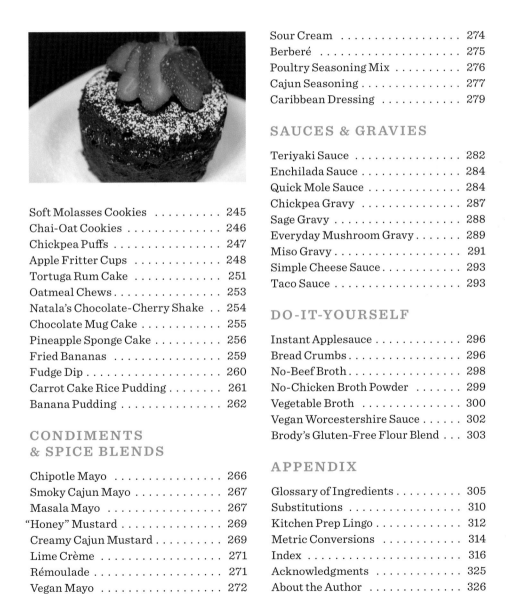

INTRODUCTION

A Word from Lindsay

Shortly after I finished my first cookbook, *The Happy Herbivore Cookbook*, my husband and I were transferred to St. Maarten for a year. While the prospect of living in paradise was quite exciting, the realization that I'd have to cook three meals a day, *every* day, was daunting.

Prepared and prepackaged vegan foods are not available in St. Maarten and the local restaurants generally do not have vegan or vegan-friendly options either. The reality was, if we were going to eat, I had to make it myself.

Living in St. Maarten reminded me how beautiful (and delicious!) simplicity can be. I needed meals that were fresh, fast, and effortless to avoid feeling overwhelmed by constant cooking, but I also needed to find a way to make meals that were exciting and satisfying with whatever I had available. In St. Maarten, I didn't have the same wide variety of ingredients I enjoyed in New York City and what was available to me at the market was always changing, too.

My new streamlined "make it work" approach, however, is what led to this book. Inside you'll find more than 175 doable recipes—recipes that are so quick and easy, you could cook from scratch three meals a day, like I do, and from whatever ingredients you have on hand.

As with the last book, my recipes are still made with wholesome "everyday" ingredients and without added fats like oil. I've also taken care to make sure most of the recipes come together in under 20 minutes, because even chefs don't always want to toil over a hot stove all day.

Why Vegan?

Eating a plant-based diet is the nation's fastest-growing food trend, and for good reason. The more plant-based meals we eat, the more benefits we will feel and bestow. Whenever someone asks me why I'm a vegan, I reply, "For my health, my pocketbook, the animals, the environment . . . and for you."

HEALTH: A vegan diet has zero dietary cholesterol, and a low-fat vegan diet also tends to be low in calories but high in fiber. Some studies have also shown that eating a low-fat vegan diet can prevent, cure, and reverse devastating diseases like hypertension, diabetes, and cancer.

WALLETS: A vegan diet can be a bargain. Vegan staples like beans, rice, and nondairy milks cost a fraction of the price of meats and dairy products. Plus, eating healthfully will save you on health-care costs in the long run.

ANIMALS: The lives and deaths of farm animals are often horrifyingly brutal, both physically and psychologically. As a consumer picking up the end product, it's easy to be oblivious rather than conscious.

ENVIRONMENT: A vegan diet is the most eco-friendly and sustainable way we can eat.

HUMANITY: It has been said that if the world went vegetarian, we would almost immediately end world hunger. One acre of land can produce either 20,000 pounds of potatoes or a measly 165 pounds of meat.

MY STORY: I was a vegetarian for most of my childhood out of a love for animals—I was eating a burger one day in the car as we drove past grazing cows and when I put it together, that was that. But I fell into a meat-eating lifestyle in my teens due to peer pressure. A serious health scare in my early twenties brought me back to a vegetarian diet, and I went vegan the following year as an experiment.

After reading *The China Study*, *Eat to Live*, and *Skinny Bitch* I knew I could never go back to vegetarianism. I made my vegan regimen permanent, with a new addition: a diet that not only cut out meat, dairy, and eggs, but one that was low-fat and based on whole foods.

Why Fat-Free and Low-Fat?

Like many others, my husband and I both struggled with our weight and health for years. In 2007 I adopted a low-fat, no-added-fat vegan diet, and Scott joined me shortly thereafter. In the span of a year, we both lost more weight than we previously thought possible and reversed or eliminated all of our medical conditions. We also noticed a surge in our energy levels and went on to complete our first marathon, something that never seemed realistic or possible before.

We all know about the dangers of hydrogenated oils, but other oils, like olive oil, can also be harmful. Most "cooking oils," such as canola oil, have very low burning points. When these oils are heated beyond that boiling point, the nutrients are lost and free radicals are created. Oils are also sneaky calorie bombs, both high in fat and high in calories. One tablespoon of oil has approximately 120 calories and 14g of fat—the same as a candy bar!

To obtain essential fatty acids, I eat unprocessed fats such as nuts and seeds sparingly. Also remember that all foods, even greens, naturally contain a little fat, so the body is always getting plenty of fat without adding extra.

The nutritional information for each recipe was computed using caloriecount.com. Each analysis provided is per serving. Unless otherwise noted, optional ingredients are not included. Breads and wraps are also not included, unless specifically noted (see packaging for that information). Sodium content is not included because the value changes significantly between brands and the calculator tools have too much discrepancy with sodium to provide a safe estimate.

Getting Started

Most of the ingredients in this cookbook can be found in any supermarket, but a select few will require a trip to the health food store or, if you prefer, placing an order online. If you are new to vegan food, whole foods, or low-fat cooking, some of the ingredients in this cookbook might be unfamiliar to you, so check the Glossary of Ingredients (pg. 305) to learn about them and where you can find them for the lowest price.

SHOPPING LIST

Below is my basic shopping list. If you have these ingredients on hand you can make almost anything in this cookbook without making a special trip to the grocery store. I highly recommend buying low-sodium and/or no-salt-added items whenever possible, particularly with canned goods such as tomatoes or beans, low-sodium soy sauce, and vegetable broth. I also recommend selecting organic and unsweetened varieties and avoiding items that contain refined sugar, high-fructose corn syrup, fat (particularly hydrogenated fats), and anything that's not vegan (contains dairy, meat, eggs, fish, or animal by-products such as gelatin, casein, or whey).

PANTRY:

agave nectar	high-heat cooking spray such as coconut or safflower	Tetra-packed shelf-stable tofu such as Mori-Nu
almond extract		
baking powder	instant oats	tomato paste
baking soda	marinara sauce	tomato sauce
balsamic vinegar	old-fashioned rolled oats	tomatoes, canned
brown rice	onions	unsweetened applesauce
brown sugar	pure maple syrup	unsweetened cocoa
chickpea flour	pure pumpkin, canned	vanilla extract
confectioners' sugar	quinoa	vegetable broth and/or vegetable bouillon cubes
distilled white vinegar	raisins	
dried and/or canned beans	raw sugar	vital wheat gluten
dried lentils and split peas	salsas	whole-wheat or brown rice pasta
garlic	smooth peanut butter	
green chiles, canned	sweet potatoes or yams	yellow cornmeal

REFRIGERATOR:

barbecue sauce
carrots
celery
corn tortillas
Dijon mustard
firm and extra-firm tofu
fresh ginger root

hot sauce such as Tabasco
ketchup
lemon juice
lettuce or salad mixes
lime juice
low-sodium soy sauce
nondairy milks

nutritional yeast
prepared yellow mustard
fresh fruits and vegetables
whole-wheat breads
    and tortillas

FREEZER:

frozen bananas
frozen berries

mixed vegetables
white whole-wheat flour

whole-wheat buns & breads
yellow corn

SPICES:

black pepper
chili powder
chipotle powder
dried marjoram
    and/or oregano
dried rosemary
dried thyme
garam masla

garlic powder (granulated)
ground cinnamon
ground coriander
ground cumin
ground nutmeg
fine sea salt
Italian seasoning
mild curry powder

onion powder (granulated)
paprika
pumpkin pie spice
red pepper flakes
rubbed sage (not powdered)
turmeric

Tools are important, too. You'll need pots and pans, a sharp knife, mixing bowls, measuring cups and spoons, at least one cutting board, a baking sheet, a whisk and spatula, a strainer, grater, mortar and pestle, and a food processor or blender.

Everyday Cooking Tips

Cook a big pot of brown rice or quinoa on the weekend so you always have a prepared grain on hand to complete a meal.

Invest in an electric steamer (about $20). Steamers save time by allowing you to cook your veggies passively in the background while you prepare other meal components.

Have backup plans. I keep tofu and black beans on hand; if all else fails, I can make Tofu Scramble (pg. 28) or Quick Burgers (pg. 81)

Plan a week's worth of meals, purchase necessary ingredients, and keep your list on the fridge.

For faster and more uniform chopping, hold the blade in front of the handle, rather than on the handle.

Do bulk prep, such as chopping vegetables, on the weekend or at night when you're watching TV.

Remember that every meal doesn't have to be complicated; simple is good, too.

Keep a well-stocked pantry, freezer, and spice rack.

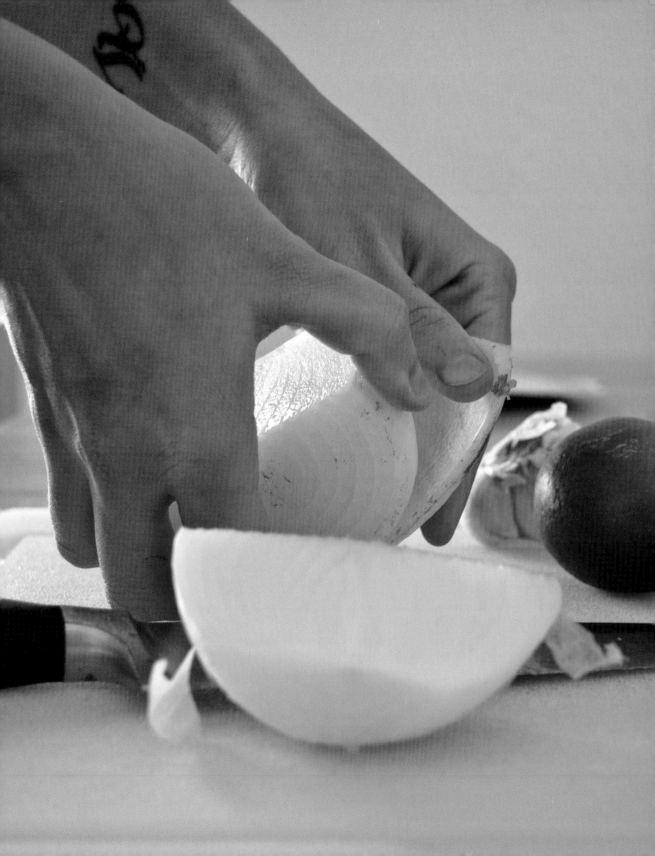

How to Use This Book

30 **QUICK:** Recipes that can be made, start to finish, in 30 minutes or less. Some recipes may require multitasking to complete in 30 minutes.

F **FAT-FREE:** Recipes with less than 1 gram of fat per serving.

G **GLUTEN-FREE:** Recipes that don't require whole-wheat flours, vital wheat gluten, seitan, or barley. I can't vouch for all the ingredients, so if you have an allergy, please make sure every ingredient you use (e.g., low-sodium soy sauce, spices, or oats) is a certified gluten-free brand. You can also substitute tamari for low-sodium soy sauce.

S **SOY-FREE:** Recipes that don't require tofu, low-sodium soy sauce, or other soy products. If the recipe calls for nondairy milk, you can make it soy-free by using almond, hemp, or rice milk, or another soy-free option. Use chickpea miso in recipes calling for miso to make it soy-free.

ONE-POT MEAL: Meals that are prepared using only one pot or baking dish.

MAKE AHEAD: Recipes where all or a portion can be done ahead of time to expedite cooking on a weeknight.

$ **BUDGET:** Recipes that cost roughly $5 or less to make with a well-stocked pantry and spice rack.

1 **SINGLE SERVING:** Recipes that serve one person.

RECIPES

Smoothies, Yogurts, & Granola

Oh She Glows Oats

Serves 1 | Angela Liddon, the fabulous gal behind the popular blog Oh She Glows (ohsheglows.com), created this recipe. Angela calls it "overnight oats," but the texture is more like a creamy yogurt once it's set.

1½ tbsp chia seeds
¾ c nondairy milk
¼ c rolled oats
1 banana, sliced

1. In a glass bowl, mix chia seeds with nondairy milk and rolled oats.

2. Cover with plastic wrap (optional) and place in fridge, allowing it to set overnight.

3. Give it a good stir in the morning, then top with banana slices, or any other topping you like. (Angela likes to add fresh sliced strawberries or a dab of peanut or almond butter to hers.)

CHEF'S NOTE: For a low-fat and low-calorie "overnight oats" option, I sometimes soak the oats in water without chia seeds. Try 1/3 cup oats with 2/3 cup water.

CHEF'S NOTE: Although chia seeds aren't an "everyday" or fat-free ingredient, I splurge on them from time to time since they're rich in omega 3-fatty acids and a good source of protein, potassium, and calcium. You can find chia seeds, also called Salba (a brand name), at health food stores or online.

NUTRITIONAL INFORMATION 350 Calories, **8.6g** Fat, **60.4g** Carbohydrates, **14.1g** Fiber, **24g** Sugars, **14.7g** Protein

Peanut Butter Cup Smoothie ③⓪

Serves 1 | *Pictured opposite* | This is hands down the most popular smoothie recipe on Happyherbivore.com. It's a "cheater" recipe since it uses a little peanut butter, but you can substitute peanut flour to taste for a lower-fat option.

2 frozen bananas
1 tbsp smooth peanut
    butter
1 tbsp unsweetened cocoa
¼ c nondairy milk

1. Combine all ingredients in a blender and whiz until smooth, adding more nondairy milk as necessary.

Banana Frosty ③⓪ Ⓖ Ⓢ $ ❶

Serves 1 | It whips up in seconds and tastes just like the famous Frosty at Wendy's—only this is a lot healthier and made from bananas.

2 frozen bananas
1 tbsp unsweetened cocoa
¼ c nondairy milk
¼ tsp vanilla extract
¼ tsp ground cinnamon

1. Place all ingredients together in a strong blender or food processor and whiz until smooth, creamy, and thick like a Frosty, adding more liquid if necessary.

2. Taste, adding more cocoa if desired (depending on the ripeness of your banana, you may need to add a little, or a lot more to get a rich chocolate flavor).

CHEF'S NOTE:
Spotted and very
ripe bananas work
best here.

CHEF'S NOTE: For an ice-cream consistency, use less liquid and a food processor.

NUTRITIONAL INFORMATION

PEANUT BUTTER CUP SMOOTHIE 334 Calories, 10.1g Fat, 65g Carbohydrates, 9g Fiber, 31.9g Sugars, 9.1g Protein

BANANA FROSTY 217 Calories, 1.5g Fat, 52.7g Carbohydrates, 7.3g Fiber, 28.1g Sugars, 5.3g Protein

Tofu Yogurt 30 F G ⏰ $

Serves 2 | I love a bowl of cold vegan yogurt piled high with fresh fruit for breakfast, but hate how expensive (and high in sugar!) most commercial vegan yogurts can be. I always keep a box or two of Mori-Nu tofu in my fridge so I can make yogurt quickly in the morning when I'm not in the mood for a hot breakfast or a smoothie. Add rolled oats and fresh fruit for texture and to create a parfait.

1 12.3-oz pkg Mori-Nu
   tofu (any firmness)
1 cold banana
2 tbsp nondairy milk
2 tbsp lemon juice
2 tbsp sweetener
   (optional)

1. Combine tofu, banana, nondairy milk, and lemon juice in a blender or food processor and whiz until smooth and creamy.

2. Taste, adding sweetener such as maple syrup or agave nectar to taste. I like to leave the yogurt unsweetened (it reminds me of Greek yogurt) and drizzle with agave nectar over top.

CHEF'S NOTE: Add fresh or frozen fruit (such as strawberries or blueberries), ¼ cup at a time, for fruit-flavored yogurts.

CHEF'S NOTE: Bananas turn brown when they oxidize, meaning the yogurt will turn brown if you make it ahead and leave it in the fridge. It hasn't gone bad, it just doesn't look pretty. If you do a fruit flavor, however, you usually can't notice the color change. You can also blend without the banana and reblend with the banana before serving to keep the color white.

CHEF'S NOTE: Probiotics can be purchased at health food stores and added to your homemade yogurt.

NUTRITIONAL INFORMATION

UNSWEETENED **128** Calories, **1.4g** Fat, **17.3g** Carbohydrates, **1.6g** Fiber, **9.1g** Sugars, **13.4g** Protein

SWEETENED **192** Calories, **1.4g** Fat, **34.6g** Carbohydrates, **1.6g** Fiber, **26.3g** Sugars, **13.5g** Protein

Hot Breakfasts & Brunch

Mexican Scramble 30 G ⬭ $

Serves 2 | I dreamed this recipe into life—literally. I woke up one morning with a vivid recollection that I'd made this exact recipe in my dream and wouldn't you know it, I had all the ingredients on hand! Now I make this scramble for breakfast any time I have leftover Enchilada Sauce!

1 lb firm or extra-firm tofu
3 tbsp nutritional yeast
1 tbsp Dijon mustard
1 tsp onion powder
   (granulated)
1 tsp garlic powder
   (granulated)
1 tsp chili powder
½ tsp ground coriander
½ tsp ground cumin
¼ tsp turmeric
1 tbsp nondairy milk
½ c sliced cherry tomatoes
¼ c fresh chopped
   cilantro (optional)
¼ c Enchilada Sauce
   (pg. 284)
hot sauce (optional)

1. Drain excess water from tofu.
2. Add to the skillet and turn heat to medium.
3. Using a spatula, break tofu into chunks, then add nutritional yeast, mustard, and spices, stirring to combine. As you stir, break down the tofu more so it looks like scrambled eggs. (A potato masher works great for this, too.)
4. Cook for 2 to 3 minutes, until the tofu turns yellow and is warm.
5. Add a splash of nondairy milk if necessary to prevent sticking.
6. Add tomatoes and cilantro on top and cook for another minute or so, until tomatoes soften slightly.
7. Season with salt and pepper. (I like a lot of both!)
8. Plate scramble and spoon warm Enchilada Sauce over the top. Serve with hot sauce on the table.

CHEF'S NOTE: For soft and "wet" scrambled eggs, use firm tofu; otherwise, use extra-firm tofu.

CHEF'S NOTE: Tomato-based salsa can be substituted for the Enchilada Sauce in a pinch. Additionally, leftover pinto or black beans make a great addition and help extend the servings.

NUTRITIONAL INFORMATION ⬭ **175** Calories, **3.3g** Fat, **15.9g** Carbohydrates, **5.8g** Fiber, **4.2g** Sugars, **24.5g** Protein

Basic Tofu Scramble 30 G ⬭ $

Serves 2 | Pictured on pg. 24 | This is my go-to meal for breakfast, lunch, and dinner when I don't have much on hand or I'm in no mood to cook. It comes together quickly and it's my favorite way to eat tofu. Plus it's a great blank canvas, meaning you can add whatever beans and vegetables you have on hand.

1 lb firm or extra-firm
   tofu, drained
3 tbsp nutritional yeast
1 tbsp Dijon mustard
1 tsp garlic powder
   (granulated)
1 tsp onion powder
   (granulated)
¼ tsp turmeric
½ tsp ground cumin
nondairy milk or water,
   as needed
salt or black salt, to taste
black pepper, to taste

1. Place tofu in a nonstick skillet and break apart into large chunks with a spatula.

2. Cook over medium-high heat until tofu releases its water, about 3 to 4 minutes.

3. Add remaining ingredients, stirring to coat evenly. Break up any large remaining chunks until the tofu is crumbly and looks like scrambled eggs. (A potato masher works great for this, too.)

4. Continue to cook, stirring regularly, until all water has evaporated—about 10 minutes.

5. Mix in prepared and cooked vegetables and beans, if using, and continue to cook until everything is thoroughly warmed.

6. Add a splash of water or nondairy milk if necessary to prevent sticking.

7. Add salt (or black salt for a really eggy taste) and pepper as desired and serve immediately. (I like my "eggs" rather salty and peppery!)

NUTRITIONAL INFORMATION 🥄 **121** Calories, **2.3g** Fat, **7.1g** Carbohydrates, **1.8g** Fiber, **1.8g** Sugars, **18.9g** Protein

CHEF'S NOTE: Black salt is a pungent-smelling purplish rock salt and is the secret ingredient here for getting tofu to taste like eggs. You can find black salt at an Indian grocery store or in your supermarket if they have a Middle Eastern or Indian section. Black salt can also be found in spice shops and online. If you can't find black salt, substitute a pinch of sea salt in its place. The taste won't be the same, but it will do.

CHEF'S NOTE: Anytime I have leftover tomato sauce, I add ¼ to ½ cup of it to my tofu scramble, depending on how much tomato flavor I want. I also tend to increase the nutritional yeast by a tablespoon or two when I do this—I find together they give the scramble a bit of a cheddary flavor.

CHEF'S NOTE: For a soy-free scramble, substitute 1 head of cauliflower for the tofu, using the shredding and cooking process in the Cheesy Cauliflower Hash (pg. 233). It's not identical to tofu scramble, but it's still a great alternative.

CHEF'S NOTE: Leftover scramble makes an awesome breakfast pizza. Spread a little pizza sauce or marinara on the surface of a whole-wheat pita. Top with scramble and any other toppings you desire. Gently heat on warm in your toaster oven.

Charleston Grits 30 F G S $ 1

Serves 1 | When I lived in Charleston, SC, I fell in love with the city's signature dish, shrimp and grits, and have been trying to re-create it since going vegan. After many ill attempts, I decided to borrow the flavors and apply them to the grits alone, rather than fuss with making a shrimp analogue. The result was perfect—and so simple it was criminal.

1 c water
¼ c quick grits
1 tbsp nutritional yeast
¼ tsp Cajun Seasoning
    (pg. 277)
salt and pepper, to taste

1. Bring water to a boil and slowly stir in grits.
2. Reduce heat to low and continue to cook, stirring occasionally until all the water is gone and the grits are thick like oatmeal, about 5 minutes.
3. If the grits get too thick, add a little hot water to thin out.
4. Add nutritional yeast and Cajun Seasoning, stirring to combine.
5. Taste, adding salt and pepper or more Cajun Seasoning as desired, and serve.

> **CHEF'S NOTE:** "Quick grits" are grits that cook in 5 minutes. If you can't find quick grits, use regular grits but note that the cooking time will be longer (see the back of the box for instructions).

NUTRITIONAL INFORMATION **65** Calories, **1g** Fat, **10.5g** Carbohydrates, **3.5g** Fiber, **0.8g** Sugars, **5.2g** Protein

Spinach & Artichoke Frittata

Serves 4 | I was addicted to spinach and artichoke dip in my pre-vegan days and had a hunch these two ingredients would make a fabulous frittata. They sure do! This dish is delicious and requires so little effort. It also presents beautifully, making it ideal for brunch with family and friends.

2 12.3-oz pkg Mori-Nu tofu
¼ c nutritional yeast
¼ c cornstarch
1 tsp salt
1½ tsp garlic powder (granulated)
1½ tsp onion powder (granulated)
1 tbsp Dijon mustard
1¼ tsp Italian seasoning
¼ tsp turmeric
1 14-oz can artichoke hearts, drained and quartered
3 to 4 c coarsely chopped spinach

1. Preheat oven to 375°F.
2. Grease an 8-inch square or round pan and set aside.
3. Put tofu, nutritional yeast, cornstarch, salt, garlic powder, onion powder, and mustard in a blender or food processor and puree until smooth and creamy, stopping to scrape sides as necessary.
4. Transfer to a mixing bowl and mix in Italian seasoning and turmeric.
5. Stir in artichoke hearts and spinach; mix until well combined.
6. Pour batter into prepared baking dish and bake for 45 minutes to 1 hour, or until thoroughly cooked through to the middle and the top is firm and golden.

Make Ahead You can make this Frittata ahead of time and gently reheat it in a warm oven or serve it at room temperature as a "quiche."

CHEF'S NOTE: All Mori-Nu tofu is essentially the same, and any firmness can be used here.

CHEF'S NOTE: A special thanks to Alicia Simpson, author of *Vegan Celebrations*, who showed me how to make frittatas with Mori-Nu tofu.

NUTRITIONAL INFORMATION 148 Calories, 1.9g Fat, 20.5g Carbohydrates, 6.7g Fiber, 2g Sugars, 13.6 Protein

Mexican Frittata

Serves 6 | At La Samanna, where I consulted as a vegan chef in St. Maarten, I developed a recipe for spicy red pepper mini tofu quiches that everyone just loves. I borrowed the flavor from that recipe and applied it to this frittata, adding beans to make it a more balanced meal.

2 12.3-oz pkg Mori-Nu tofu
3 tbsp nutritional yeast
4 tbsp cornstarch
1 tsp sea salt
1½ tsp garlic powder (granulated)
1½ tsp onion powder (granulated)
1 tbsp Dijon mustard
1 tsp Old Bay seasoning
1 red bell pepper, seeded and diced
1½ c black beans
¼ c cilantro, chopped (optional)

1. Preheat oven to 375°F.
2. Grease an 8- or 9-inch square or round pan.
3. Place tofu, nutritional yeast, cornstarch, salt, garlic powder, onion powder, and mustard in a blender or food processor and puree until smooth and creamy, stopping to scrape sides as necessary.
4. Transfer to a mixing bowl and mix with Old Bay seasoning. If the mixture doesn't look speckled, add more Old Bay seasoning (more is better than less: be generous), and set aside.
5. Stir in red bell pepper, beans, and cilantro, if using.
6. Bake for 45 minutes, or until golden across the top and thoroughly cooked in the middle.

Make Ahead You can prepare this quiche up to 12 hours in advance. Cover it with plastic wrap and store it in the fridge until you're ready to bake it.

> **CHEF'S NOTE:** Since all Mori-Nu tofu is fairly similar in terms of firmness, any can be used, but the firmer, the better.

> **CHEF'S NOTE:** A special thanks to Alicia Simpson, author of *Vegan Celebrations*, who showed me how to make frittatas with Mori-Nu tofu.

NUTRITIONAL INFORMATION 380 Calories, 2.2g Fat, 67.9g Carbohydrates, 12.2g Fiber, 4.5g Sugars, 24.8g Protein

OK, not great but good enuf to make again!

Marmalade French Toast Ⓕ Ⓢ Ⓘ $

Serves 2 | Most mornings I'm in no mood to fuss with cooking of any kind—even oatmeal feels too cumbersome. Enter this French toast. It takes minutes to whip up the night before. And then the morning of? All you need to do is pop it in the oven. It's so easy and totally worth the little forethought required. You want to use hearty whole-wheat or multi-grain bread slices here.

¾ c nondairy milk

2 tbsp chickpea flour

1 tsp ground cinnamon

¼ tsp salt

¼ cup apricot marmalade

6 slices of whole-wheat
  or multi-grain bread,
  sliced diagonally

pure maple syrup,
  for dipping

fresh fruit topping
  (optional)

1. If using a baguette instead of sandwich bread, cut diagonally into ½-inch thickness.

2. Whisk or blend nondairy milk with flour, cinnamon, salt, and marmalade until well combined into a thin liquid.

3. Lightly grease a 13 x 9-inch casserole dish and line with your bread slices. Completely cover the bottom of the dish. A little overlap is fine, but just a little.

4. Pour mixture over the top, making sure every piece is well and evenly coated.

5. Cover with plastic wrap and refrigerate overnight.

6. In the morning, preheat oven to 350°F.

7. Garnish the bread with a few sprinkles of cinnamon, and bake for 20 to 30 minutes, or until your bread is golden brown and somewhat crusty and warm.

8. Serve with pure maple syrup and fresh fruit (if desired).

CHEF'S NOTE: Chopped pecans or walnuts make a nice addition. If serving this at brunch, also consider adding sliced strawberries on top for added color and presentation.

CHEF'S NOTE: Any light-colored marmalade such as peach, orange, or apricot will work here. Don't use heavy and dark-colored marmalade like blackberry or grape.

NUTRITIONAL INFORMATION (WITH WHOLE-WHEAT BREAD) 🍞 **384** Calories, **3.7g** Fat, **73.5g** Carbohydrates, **8.6g** Fiber, **28.1g** Sugars, **16.7g** Protein

Carrot Cake Pancakes

Makes 6 | I don't know why I never thought until now to blend my love for carrot cake with my love for pancakes. These pancakes take the cake—literally! And they add a vegetable to breakfast. That's what I like to call a win-win!

1 c white whole-wheat flour
1 tbsp baking powder
pinch of salt
½ tsp ground cinnamon
dash of ground cloves
dash of ground ginger
2 tsp light brown sugar (optional)
½ c nondairy milk
½ c water
¼ c shredded carrots
pure maple syrup, for dipping

1. In a mixing bowl, whisk flour, baking powder, salt, and spices together.
2. Add brown sugar if using, nondairy milk, and water, and stir to combine.
3. Let batter rest for 10 minutes.
4. Meanwhile grate carrots as finely as possible and heat a nonstick skillet or spritz a frying pan with cooking spray. When a drop of water fizzles on the skillet, it's ready.
5. Turn heat down to low and mix carrot pieces into your batter.
6. Pour pancake batter ¼ cup at a time into skillet. Cook on one side until bubbles form, about 2 minutes, then gently flip and cook for another 2 to 3 minutes. Repeat, remixing batter between each pancake since the carrot pieces tend to sink down.
7. Serve with pure maple syrup.

CHEF'S NOTE: As an alternative to maple syrup, mix vegan cream cheese with a drop or two of vanilla extract, a dash of cinnamon, a little powdered sugar (optional; to taste), and nondairy milk until it has a runnier consistency.

NUTRITIONAL INFORMATION (1 PANCAKE, WITHOUT MAPLE SYRUP)
79 Calories, **0.4g** Fat, **16.8g** Carbohydrates, **2.3g** Fiber, **1.9g** Sugars, **3.4g** Protein

Dark Chocolate Pancakes

Makes 6 | These chocolate pancakes remind me of Black Forest cake, since they have a strong dark-chocolate flavor and are served with fruity jam instead of maple syrup.

¾ c whole-wheat pastry flour
¼ c unsweetened cocoa
1 tbsp baking powder
pinch of salt
1 c nondairy milk
2 tbsp agave nectar
2 tbsp raw sugar (optional)
strawberry or raspberry jam

1. Whisk flour, cocoa, baking powder and salt together in a large bowl.
2. Combine nondairy milk with agave nectar and sugar, if using.
3. Pour wet mixture into dry mixture and stir until just combined; a few lumps are okay.
4. Let rest for 10 minutes.
5. Meanwhile, heat a skillet over very low heat.
6. Transfer mixture to a large glass/liquid measuring cup or use a greased ¼-cup measuring cup.
7. Spray skillet with cooking spray and pour ¼ cup of batter for each pancake.
8. Cook on one side until bubbles form, then gently flip and cook for another 2 to 3 minutes.
9. Serve with jam.

CHEF'S NOTE: A delicious, though not fat-free option, is to serve these pancakes with a little peanut butter warmed in the microwave so it's runny, and topped with fresh banana slices.

NUTRITIONAL INFORMATION (1 PANCAKE, PLAIN) **101** Calories, **0.8g** Fat, **21.9g** Carbohydrates, **2.8g** Fiber, **7.9g** Sugars, **3.6g** Protein

Muffins, Biscuits, & Breads

Chocolate Spice Muffins

Makes 12 | As I was licking the batter for my basic chocolate muffin recipe, I wondered what I could put in it to make it different. My mind kept coming back to garam masala, but the combination just seemed too weird. Eventually I thought, "To hell with it!" and gave it a try. The result? Outstanding. These muffins are incredible and the flavor will keep people guessing!

1¾ c whole-wheat pastry flour
¼ c unsweetened cocoa
1 tbsp baking powder
¼ tsp salt
½ c brown or raw sugar
1 to 1½ tsp garam masala
½ c unsweetened applesauce
½ c nondairy milk
¼ cup water
1 tsp vanilla extract

1. In a mixing bowl, whisk flour, cocoa, baking powder, salt, and sugar together (for a sweet muffin, add another ¼ cup sugar).

2. Stir in 1 to 1½ teaspoons of garam masala, using the lesser amount if your blend is very strong and potent.

3. Add applesauce, nondairy milk, water, and vanilla, and stir until just combined.

4. Set batter aside and preheat oven to 350°F.

5. Grease a muffin tin and spoon batter into cups ¾ full.

6. Bake for 15 to 20 minutes, or until a toothpick inserted in the center comes out clean.

> **CHEF'S NOTE:** These muffins are very light and fluffy and not as moist as my muffins tend to be. For a moister muffin, add another ¼ cup of applesauce.

NUTRITIONAL INFORMATION (1 MUFFIN) **101** Calories, **0.6g** Fat, **22g** Carbohydrates, **2.5g** Fiber, **7.5g** Sugars, **2.5g** Protein

French Toast Muffins

Makes 12 | *Pictured opposite and on pg. 24* | Finally, a portable French toast! These muffins are *deeelicious* and my favorite morning treat.

1¾ c whole-wheat
    pastry flour
1 tbsp baking powder
½ c light brown or raw
    sugar
¼ tsp salt
1 tbsp ground cinnamon
dash of ground nutmeg
1 c nondairy milk
¼ c chickpea flour
1 tsp vanilla or maple
    extract
¼ c unsweetened
    applesauce
oats (optional)

1. Preheat oven to 350°F.
2. Grease a muffin tin or spray paper liners to prevent sticking and set aside.
3. In a mixing bowl, whisk whole-wheat flour, baking powder, sugar (for a sweet muffin, add another ¼ cup of sugar), salt, cinnamon, and a dash or two of nutmeg together until well combined.
4. In a small bowl, whisk nondairy milk with chickpea flour and extract.
5. Pour on top of flour mixture, add applesauce, and stir until just combined.
6. Spoon into muffin cups ¾ full and sprinkle with oats and extra brown sugar on top, if desired.
7. Bake for 15 to 25 minutes, or until a toothpick inserted in the center comes out clean.

CHEF'S NOTE:
These muffins are very light and fluffy and not as moist as my muffins tend to be. For a moister muffin, add another ¼ cup of applesauce.

CHEF'S NOTE: Drizzle a little maple syrup on the muffins once they've cooled slightly for an even more authentic French toast taste. You can also smear a little maple on the muffins as you would with jam or margarine.

NUTRITIONAL INFORMATION (1 MUFFIN) **113** Calories, **0.6g** Fat, **23.4g** Carbohydrates, **2.8g** Fiber, **7.4g** Sugars, **3.3g** Protein

Morning Glory Muffins G

Makes 12 | These muffins are a meal full of whole grains, protein, vegetables, and fruits. Starting your day off right has never tasted so good!

1½ c oat flour
2 tsp baking powder
1 tsp baking soda
1 tsp pumpkin pie spice
½ tsp salt
⅓ to ½ c raisins
1 c baby carrots, shredded
6 oz silken tofu
2 tbsp nondairy milk
½ c canned pure pumpkin
⅓ c Medjool dates
1 tsp vanilla extract
¼ c light brown sugar
   (optional)

1. To make oat flour, whiz instant or rolled oats in your blender until they reach a flourlike consistency.

2. Combine 1½ cups of oat flour with baking powder, baking soda, pumpkin pie spice, and salt in a mixing bowl.

3. Stir in raisins and carrots and set aside.

4. In a blender, combine tofu, nondairy milk, pumpkin, dates, vanilla, and sugar if using. Puree until smooth and creamy, stopping to scrape the sides as necessary.

5. Pour into flour mixture and stir until just combined.

6. Let batter rest while you preheat the oven to 350°F.

7. Grease a muffin tin or spray liners to prevent sticking.

8. Spoon in batter to ¾ full and bake for 18 to 25 minutes, or until a toothpick inserted in the center comes out clean.

CHEF'S NOTE:
½ package of Mori-Nu tofu (any firmness) can be substituted for the silken tofu.

CHEF'S NOTE: Use the full ½ cup of raisins if you're omitting the sugar. Chopped raw walnut pieces also make a nice addition to these muffins.

NUTRITIONAL INFORMATION

1 MUFFIN (WITH SUGAR) 99 Calories, **1.6g** Fat, **19.7g** Carbohydrates, **2.2g** Fiber, **9.1g** Sugars, **3g** Protein

1 MUFFIN (NO SUGAR, EXTRA RAISINS) 94 Calories, **1.6g** Fat, **18.5g** Carbohydrates, **2.2g** Fiber, **7.5g** Sugars, **3g** Protein

Single Blueberry Muffin 30 F S $ 1

Serves 1 | I really love warm muffins fresh out of the oven for breakfast, but anytime I bake a batch, I run the risk of eating the entire pan by nightfall. Now I can have a muffin, and not eat two! Or three! (Or four!)

3 tbsp whole-wheat
   pastry flour
1 tbsp raw sugar
1 tbsp agave nectar
1 tbsp nondairy milk
¼ tsp baking powder
1½ tbsp blueberries,
   rinsed
¼ tsp lemon or vanilla
   extract

1. Preheat oven or toaster oven to 350°F.
2. Grease a single muffin cup or place a baking liner in a metal 1-cup measuring cup (or use a foil baking cup that stands up on its own), and set aside.
3. Place all ingredients in a mixing bowl, stirring to combine.
4. Transfer to cookware and bake for 15 to 20 minutes, or until a toothpick inserted in the center comes out clean.

CHEF'S NOTE: A good pinch of lemon zest may be substituted for the lemon extract.

NUTRITIONAL INFORMATION (1 MUFFIN) 203 Calories, 0.6g Fat, 48.1g Carbohydrates, 3.6g Fiber, 28.9g Sugars, 2.7g Protein

Glazed Pumpkin Biscuits

Makes 6 | These biscuits are a delicious way to use up leftover canned pumpkin. I love to serve them as a breakfast treat during the fall months.

1 c white whole-wheat
   flour
2 tsp pumpkin pie spice
1 tsp baking powder
pinch of salt
2 tbsp light brown sugar
   (optional)
¼ c canned pure pumpkin
¼ c nondairy milk
Basic Glaze (pg. 62)

1. Preheat oven to 375°F.

2. Grease a cookie sheet or line with parchment paper and set aside.

3. In a mixing bowl, whisk flour, pumpkin pie spice, baking powder, salt, and sugar together.

4. Add pumpkin and stir until small pebbles of dough form, stopping to scrape dough off your spoon. A light flour dusting is okay, but you don't want a lot of excess flour, and make sure not to stir too much—the dough balls are important.

5. Add nondairy milk, stirring to incorporate. If the batter looks dry, add a splash of nondairy milk (when in doubt, wetter is better).

6. Drop 6 equal spoonfuls onto your prepared cookie sheet and bake for 7 to 10 minutes, until firm to the touch and the bottoms are golden.

7. Meanwhile, make glaze, adding a dash of pumpkin pie spice (if desired).

8. Spoon glaze over hot biscuits and serve.

> **CHEF'S NOTE:** ⅓ to ½ cup of raisins or vegan chocolate chips make a nice addition to these biscuits.

NUTRITIONAL INFORMATION (1 BISCUIT, WITHOUT GLAZE) 🍴 **76** Calories, **0.4g** Fat, **15.7g** Carbohydrates, **2.4g** Fiber, **1.6g** Sugars, **3.1g** Protein

Cinnamon Raisin Biscuits

Makes 12 | I developed this recipe for my father. It's a copycat—but healthier version—of Hardee's famous biscuits. These biscuits are popular in my house and I tend to make them on the weekend or any morning when my fridge is looking bare.

2 c white whole-wheat
   flour
2 tsp baking powder
¼ tsp salt
1½ tsp ground cinnamon
⅓ to ½ c raisins
½ c unsweetened
   applesauce
½ c nondairy milk
Basic Glaze (pg. 62)
¼ to 1 tsp almond extract,
   for glaze

CHEF'S NOTE:
I find the raisins make these biscuits just sweet enough for my taste, but if you prefer a sweeter biscuit, add 3 tablespoons of light brown or raw sugar.

1. Preheat oven to 375°F.

2. Grease a cookie sheet or line with parchment paper and set aside.

3. In a large mixing bowl, whisk flour, baking powder, salt, and cinnamon to combine. Add raisins, stirring a few times to ensure even distribution.

4. Add applesauce and stir about 10 times, until the batter is lumpy with chunks of dough. Wipe the batter off your spoon, and stroke a few more times. A light flour dusting is okay but avoid a lot of excess flour. Also be careful not to overstir—those lumps are important.

5. Add ½ cup of nondairy milk, stirring until a wet, thick, doughy batter forms. Add another 1 to 2 tablespoons of nondairy milk, until the batter is the consistency of thick mashed potatoes (more liquid is better than less, when in doubt).

6. Drop golf-ball-size spoonfuls onto your cookie sheet, leaving a few inches between each so they can spread.

7. Bake for 12 to 15 minutes, or until golden and firm to the touch, checking after 10 minutes.

8. Meanwhile, make the glaze, replacing ¼ to 1 teaspoon of the nondairy milk with almond extract.

9. Spoon glaze over warm biscuits and serve.

NUTRITIONAL INFORMATION (1 BISCUIT, WITHOUT GLAZE) **96** Calories, **0.2g** Fat, **21.2g** Carbohydrates, **1g** Fiber, **3.9g** Sugars, **2.6g** Protein

Lemon Jam Biscuits 30 F S $

Makes 5 | We love to eat these biscuits hot out of the oven with raspberry jam, but any berry jam complements them well. They're a great alternative to regular biscuits and the lemon flavor really lightens them up—making them perfect for a spring brunch.

1 c white whole-wheat
   flour
1 tsp baking powder
½ tsp baking soda
pinch of salt
¼ c unsweetened
   applesauce
1 lemon
water

CHEF'S NOTE:
I use a lemon about the size of a hand-grip stress ball here. If you have a really big lemon you'll need to adjust the juice and zest unless you want really lemony biscuits.

1. Preheat oven to 350°F.
2. Grease a cookie sheet or line with parchment and set aside.
3. In a mixing bowl, whisk flour, baking powder, baking soda, and salt together.
4. Add applesauce, stirring until chunks and pebbles of dough form.
5. Add zest and juice of the entire lemon (squeeze it well, including using your fingers to push juice out of the fleshy parts) and stroke batter a few times.
6. Add water 1 tablespoon at a time until the batter is wet, but not so wet it's runny (about 3 tablespoons).
7. Drop 5 spoonfuls of batter onto your cookie sheet, leaving 1 inch between them. Using your fingers, form batter into flattened rounds.
8. Bake for 10 to 15 minutes, or until they are firm to the touch and the bottoms golden.
9. Slice in half and smear generously with your favorite jam.

NUTRITIONAL INFORMATION (1 BISCUIT, WITHOUT JAM) 🥄 **89** Calories, **0.4g** Fat, **19.7g** Carbohydrates, **2.7g** Fiber, **2.3g** Sugars, **3.3g** Protein

Basic Glaze

Makes ½ cup | A quick and easy universal glaze that adds a touch of sweetness to any baked good.

1 cup powdered sugar
5 tsp nondairy milk

1 Combine sugar with non-dairy milk and stir until a thick glaze forms. If its too thick, add more liquid. If its too thin, add more sugar.

> **CHEF'S NOTE:** Add or substitute for the liquid ¼ to 1 tsp of an extract, such as almond extract, or juice, such as orange juice, for a flavored glaze.

NUTRITIONAL INFORMATION (1 TBSP) **61** Calories, **0g** Fat, **15.2g** Carbohydrates, **0g** Fiber, **14.9g** Sugars, **0.1g** Protein

Harvest Cornbread

Serves 9 | In the middle of making my classic cornbread recipe I realized I was out of applesauce, so I subbed pumpkin. I figured I'd add sage and anise while I was at it and the result was extra-delicious. Cornbread with a little fall flavoring!

1 c white whole-wheat
   flour
1 c cornmeal
1 tbsp baking powder
½ tsp salt
1 to 2 tbsp minced fresh
   sage
1 c nondairy milk
¼ c canned pure pumpkin
¼ c agave nectar
2 tbsp raw sugar
   (optional)
pinch of ground anise
   (optional)

1. Preheat oven to 400°F.
2. Grease a standard 9-inch bread pan, 8-inch square baking pan, or shallow pie dish, and set aside.
3. In a large mixing bowl, whisk flour, cornmeal, baking powder, and salt together until well combined.
4. Add sage, nondairy milk, pumpkin puree, agave nectar, plus optional sugar and anise, and stir until combined.
5. Pour batter into prepared pan and bake for 20 minutes, or until a toothpick inserted in the center comes out clean and the bread is firm to the touch.

CHEF'S NOTE: If you want a strong pumpkin flavor, add several dashes of pumpkin pie spice.

NUTRITIONAL INFORMATION 🥄 **136** Calories, **0.8g** Fat, **30.3g** Carbohydrates, **2.7g** Fiber, **9.9g** Sugars, **3.9g** Protein

Bayou Cornbread

Serves 9 | My sister, Courtney, found an old family recipe for Louisiana cornbread that I just had to veganize. In Louisiana, cornbread isn't traditionally sweetened since it's supposed to go with other foods like a plain cracker. This savory cornbread is great for nibbling and broken into NOLA Gumbo (pg. 108). Thanks, Mama Ginny & Grandma Edith!

1 c nondairy milk
1 tsp lemon juice
½ c coarse cornmeal
½ c fine cornmeal
2 tbsp cornstarch
1½ tbsp whole-wheat flour
2 tsp baking powder
¼ tsp salt

1. Mix nondairy milk and lemon juice together and set aside for 10 minutes.

2. Meanwhile, in a mixing bowl, whisk cornmeals with cornstarch, flour, baking powder, and salt (you can add more salt if you like a salty bread) until well combined.

3. Preheat oven to 400°F.

4. Grease an 8- or 9-inch pan or cast-iron skillet and put it into the oven to heat for a few minutes (this is how you crisp the sides to be golden).

5. Add nondairy milk to the cornmeal mixture and stir until well combined.

6. Carefully remove hot pan from the oven and pour the batter straight in.

7. Bake for 15 to 20 minutes, or until firm to the touch and golden.

CHEF'S NOTE:
You can grind coarse cornmeal into a fine or finer cornmeal in your blender.

CHEF'S NOTE:
Soy milk works best in this recipe, followed by almond milk.

CHEF'S NOTE: Gluten-free flour may be substituted for the whole-wheat. Additionally, you can use another ½ cup of fine cornmeal instead of coarse, though it's more authentic with little grainy corn bits in the bread!

NUTRITIONAL INFORMATION 🥄 **71** Calories, **0.5g** Fat, **15g** Carbohydrates, **1.1g** Fiber, **1.5g** Sugars, **2.1g** Protein

Jalapeño Cornbread 30 F S $

Serves 9 | *Pictured on pg. 48* | This cornbread is a quick and easy side dish that takes any meal from ordinary to zesty and extraordinary. Make up a batch ahead of time, or simply place it in the oven to bake before you start prepping the main entrée, to save time.

1 c cornmeal

1 c whole-wheat pastry flour

1 tbsp baking powder

½ tsp sea salt

1 c nondairy milk

¼ c unsweetened applesauce

¼ c agave nectar

2 tbsp raw sugar (optional)

1 c yellow corn (fresh, frozen, or canned)

1 tbsp minced jalapeño

1. Preheat oven to 400°F.

2. Whisk cornmeal, flour, baking powder, and salt together in a large bowl.

3. Add nondairy milk, applesauce, agave nectar, and sugar, if using, on top.

4. With a spatula, stir a few times, then add corn and jalapeño.

5. Stir until just combined, then pour batter into a greased or nonstick 8- or 9-inch shallow pie dish, cast-iron skillet, or square casserole dish.

6. Bake for approximately 20 minutes, or until a toothpick inserted in the center comes out clean.

CHEF'S NOTE: For a denser, more intensely corn-flavored bread, increase cornmeal to 1½ cups and reduce flour to ½ cup.

NUTRITIONAL INFORMATION ⬥ **157** Calories, **0.9g** Fat, **35g** Carbohydrates, **2g** Fiber, **10.5g** Sugars, **4g** Protein

Sandwiches, Burgers, & More

Eggless Salad 30 F G ⬜ Ⓞ

Serves 6 | *Pictured opposite and on pg. 272* | My long search for the perfect vegan "egg" salad is over. This tofu eggless salad tastes just like the original, only it's fat-free and a whole lot healthier overall.

12 oz extra-firm tofu

1 tbsp low-sodium soy sauce

1 whole celery stalk, minced

1¼ tbsp nutritional yeast

1½ tbsp Dijon mustard

2 tbsp dill relish

½ tsp ground turmeric

¼ tsp mild yellow curry powder

¼ tsp garlic powder (granulated)

¼ tsp onion powder (granulated)

½ tsp black salt

2 tbsp Vegan Mayo (pg. 272)

black pepper, to taste

1. Crumble tofu into a large mixing bowl.

2. Add remaining ingredients in order, then stir until well combined.

3. Let the mixture rest for a few minutes to allow the flavors to merge and to enhance the yellow coloring.

4. Stir again and taste, adjusting spices and black pepper as necessary.

Make Ahead ✎ This eggless salad only gets better with age. Store in an airtight container in the fridge. It should last a week before expiring.

> **CHEF'S NOTE:** If using firm (rather than extra-firm) tofu, press the tofu for at least 20 minutes to extract excess water.

> **CHEF'S NOTE:** Black salt is a pungent-smelling purplish rock salt and the secret ingredient for getting tofu to taste like eggs. You can find it at Indian grocery stores, spice shops, and online. Sea salt works in a pinch but black salt is preferable.

NUTRITIONAL INFORMATION (1 SANDWICH, WITHOUT BREAD) ✎
70 Calories, **0.7g** Fat, **3.1g** Carbohydrates, **0.8g** Fiber, **1.2g** Sugars, **5.6g** Protein

"Oyster" Po'Boys

Makes 3 | A po'boy (short for "poor boy") is a popular fried-seafood sandwich from Louisiana. I've captured the seafood element here by using oyster mushrooms and seafood seasonings. This po'boy is just as flavorful as the traditional sandwich—only much healthier. Traditionally, po'boys are served on French baguettes, but any wholesome sandwich roll can be substituted.

⅔ c cornmeal
⅓ c nondairy milk
1 tbsp cornstarch
2 tsp Old Bay seasoning
½ tsp salt
¼ tsp black pepper
dash of paprika
21 oyster mushrooms
lettuce
tomato
whole-wheat baguettes
Smoky Cajun Mayo
    (pg. 267)

CHEF'S NOTE:
You'll find oyster mushrooms seasonally at farmers markets, health food stores, and Asian grocery stores.

1. Preheat oven to 350°F. Grease a cookie sheet or line with parchment paper and set aside.

2. Process cornmeal in a blender until it is fine with a flour-like consistency. Then whisk with spices in a bowl and set aside.

3. Whisk nondairy milk with cornstarch in a small bowl and set aside.

4. Place a clean bowl next to the cornmeal mixture and the bowl with the nondairy mixture above them both, making a triangle.

5. One at a time, dip mushrooms into the nondairy mixture, then put it in the clean bowl. Use a dry hand to sprinkle cornmeal mixture over the mushroom, coating it completely. (Periodically dump out the wet cornmeal mixture from the bowl.)

6. Place coated mushrooms on baking sheet and bake for 15 to 20 minutes, flipping after 10 minutes.

Make Ahead The mushrooms can be made in advance. Store in an airtight container in the fridge and warm gently in a toaster oven (preferred) or oven before assembling sandwiches.

NUTRITIONAL INFORMATION (SANDWICH, WITHOUT THE BUN)
146 Calories, **1.4g** Fat, **28.9g** Carbohydrates, **3.3g** Fiber, **3.6g** Sugars, **7g** Protein

Grilled Cheeze

Makes 2 sandwiches | One of my husband's all-time favorite pre-vegan foods was grilled cheese, so he's been after me to make a vegan version. This sauce is ooey, gooey, and spreads thick, really capturing that grilled-cheese consistency. I love to dunk my Grilled Cheeze into a bowl of tomato soup or eat it alongside a garden salad.

⅓ c nutritional yeast
½ c nondairy milk
2 tbsp white whole-wheat flour
2 tbsp cornstarch
1 tbsp ketchup
2 tsp yellow mustard
1 tsp onion powder (granulated)
1 tsp garlic powder (granulated)
¼ tsp dried dill
4 slices of toast

① Whisk all ingredients, except toast, together in a saucepan and heat over high heat, stirring constantly until really thick. (It will get lumpy then thick.)

② Smear "cheeze" on toast and serve.

> CHEF'S NOTE: Gluten-free flour may be substituted for the whole-wheat flour.

NUTRITIONAL INFORMATION (WITHOUT BREAD) 🍞 **185** Calories, **1.8g** Fat, **31.3g** Carbohydrates, **7.5g** Fiber, **5.9g** Sugars, **15.3g** Protein

Quick Burgers 30 F G S $

Makes 4 burgers | I developed these burgers in a hotel room: they're quick, easy, and require very few ingredients. (In fact, except for the beans and a seasoning packet, I sourced all the ingredients from the complimentary "breakfast bar.") I make these burgers any time I need a super-fast meal or I'm really low on ingredients.

1 15-oz can black beans, drained and rinsed
2 tbsp ketchup
1 tbsp yellow mustard
1 tsp onion powder (granulated)
1 tsp garlic powder (granulated)
⅓ c instant oats

1. Preheat oven to 400°F.
2. Grease a cookie sheet or line with parchment paper and set aside.
3. In a mixing bowl, mash black beans with a fork until mostly pureed but with some half beans and bean parts left.
4. Stir in condiments and spices until well combined, then mix in oats.
5. Divide into 4 equal portions and shape into thin patties.
6. Bake for 10 minutes, carefully flip over, and bake for another 5 minutes, or until crusty on the outside.
7. Slap onto a bun with extra condiments and eat!

NUTRITIONAL INFORMATION (1 BURGER) **109** Calories, **0.5g** Fat, **17.6g** Carbohydrates, **3g** Fiber, **2.2g** Sugars, **5g** Protein

Masala Burgers

Makes 4 burgers | *Pictured opposite and on pg. 72* | These Indian-spiced bean burgers pack a lot of flavor into each patty. I really like them on a toasted bun, but they're also great on their own with a side of greens for a hearty low-carb dinner.

1 15-oz can kidney beans,
   drained and rinsed
½ tsp garam masala
½ tsp chili powder
½ tsp cumin
½ tsp onion powder
   (granulated)
½ tsp garlic powder
   (granulated)
3 tbsp ketchup
⅓ c instant oats
Masala Mayo (pg. 267)

1. Preheat oven to 375°F.

2. Grease a cookie sheet or line with parchment paper and set aside.

3. In a mixing bowl, mash beans with a fork until no whole beans are left but not so mashed that they're pureed like refried beans.

4. Add spices and ketchup, stirring to combine.

5. Taste. If you want a more pronounced Indian flavoring, add another ¼ teaspoon each of chili powder, garam masala, and cumin.

6. Mix in oats.

7. Divide mixture into 4 equal portions and roll into balls with clean hands. Flatten with your palms and place on your prepared baking sheet. Use your fingers to shape them into a patty.

8. Bake patties for 10 minutes, gently flip over, and bake for 8 more minutes. Spray the patties with oil spray to prevent drying, if necessary or desired. Flip a third time and bake for another 5 minutes if necessary, or until the burgers are firm.

9. Top with Masala Mayo and serve.

NUTRITIONAL INFORMATION (1 BURGER) 👅 **129** Calories, **0.9g** Fat, **24.5g** Carbohydrates, **6.6g** Fiber, **4.8g** Sugars, **6.8g** Protein

Kidney-Quinoa Burgers $

Makes 6 burgers | I love a good black bean burger, but I find kidney beans lend themselves better to a true "burger" flavor and have a better consistency. Serve these burgers on a whole-wheat bun with all the fixin's.

¼ c quinoa

½ c water

1 15-oz can kidney beans, drained and rinsed

2 tbsp barbecue sauce

2 tbsp ketchup

2 tbsp low-sodium soy sauce

1 tbsp yellow mustard

1 tsp onion powder (granulated)

1 tsp garlic powder (granulated)

1 tbsp Italian seasoning

½ tsp paprika

⅓ c vital wheat gluten

1. In a small saucepan, combine quinoa with ½ cup of water, cover and bring to a boil.

2. Once boiling, reduce heat to low and continue to cook until fluffy and all water has evaporated, about 15 minutes.

3. Meanwhile, mash beans with a fork in a mixing bowl until the consistency of refried beans.

4. Add remaining ingredients in order, plus cooked quinoa, and stir to combine.

5. Preheat oven to 450°F and line a cookie sheet with parchment paper or a greased cookie sheet.

6. Break mixture into 6 equal segments. Roll each into a ball, flatten it, and shape it into a patty using your hands.

7. Bake for 8 minutes, flip, and bake for 8 more minutes, then flip again for 5 minutes, but only if necessary. When the burgers are brown and crisp on the outside, they are done.

NUTRITIONAL INFORMATION (1 BURGER) **316** Calories, **2.1g** Fat, **53.7g** Carbohydrates, **11.6g** Fiber, **4.6g** Sugars, **22.4g** Protein

Pinto Burgers

Makes 4 burgers | Poor pinto beans: they're always taking a backseat to black beans and chickpeas, at least in my house. Although I love pinto beans as Skillet Refried Beans, I had to believe they were more than a one-hit wonder, and they sure are! These flavorful burgers are just a little spicy and go perfectly on a bun with lettuce and tomato.

1 15-oz can pinto beans,
  drained and rinsed
2 tbsp Vegan Mayo
  (pg. 272)
1 tbsp ketchup
1 tsp onion powder
  (granulated)
1 tsp garlic powder
  (granulated)
½ tsp ground cumin
½ tsp chili powder
¼ to ½ tsp chipotle
  powder
⅓ c instant oats
Chipotle Mayo (pg. 266)
  or salsa

1. Preheat oven to 375°F.
2. Grease a cookie sheet or line with parchment paper and set aside.
3. In a mixing bowl, mash beans with a fork really well, making sure no whole beans are left but some bean pieces remain.
4. Add all remaining ingredients and stir to combine.
5. Divide mixture into 4 equal portions and roll into balls with clean hands. Flatten with your palms and place on your prepared baking sheet. Use your fingers to shape them into a patty.
6. Bake for 10 minutes, gently flip over, and bake for 8 more minutes. Spray the patties with oil spray to prevent drying if necessary or desired. Flip a third time and bake for another 5 minutes if necessary, or until the burgers are firm.
7. Serve with Chipotle Mayo or salsa.

NUTRITIONAL INFORMATION (1 BURGER, WITHOUT CHIPOTLE MAYO)
126 Calories, **0.5g** Fat, **24g** Carbohydrates, **7.9g** Fiber, **3.5g** Sugars, **7.8g** Protein

Island Portobello Burgers

Makes 2 burgers | If you loved the Portobello Steaks in my first cookbook you're in for a treat with their island cousins! These mushrooms are juicy, cooked with Caribbean seasonings, and make for one satisfying "burger." A little guacamole or sliced avocado on top really makes the burgers to die for, but for a fat-free version, a slice of pineapple is a great stand-in.

¼ c water
3 tbsp balsamic vinegar
1 tbsp teriyaki sauce
pinch dried thyme
¼ tsp onion powder
   (granulated)
¼ tsp garlic powder
   (granulated)
½ tsp ground ginger
⅛ tsp mild curry powder
¼ tsp chili powder
1 tsp Dijon mustard
2 portobello mushrooms
2 whole-wheat buns
2 lettuce leaves (optional)

1. Combine all ingredients except portobellos, buns, and lettuce in a skillet, breaking up thyme between your fingers as you add it.

2. Bring mixture to a boil over high heat and add mushrooms.

3. Cook for 5 minutes, flip, and cook for 5 minutes more.

4. Continue to cook and flip until mushrooms reduce in size, turn deep brown, and are very tender (usually 10 to 15 minutes total; it's better to overcook than undercook).

5. Add more water as necessary to prevent burning or sticking.

6. Drain off excess water and dab mushrooms lightly with a paper towel—you want the mushrooms mostly dry when they hit the bun.

7. Set the mushrooms bottom side up on the buns, placing guacamole, avocado, or pineapple in the cap.

NUTRITIONAL INFORMATION (1 BURGER) **39** Calories, **0.2g** Fat, **5.7g** Carbohydrates, **1.3g** Fiber, **1.6g** Sugars, **3.8g** Protein

White Enchiladas

Makes 4 | Enchiladas blancas are one of the best-kept secrets of Mexican cuisine. Traditionally, enchiladas blancas refers to chicken enchiladas smothered in queso, instead of enchilada sauce.

2 tsp cornstarch
2 tbsp water
2½ tbsp green chiles
½ c nondairy milk
¼ c nutritional yeast
1 tsp yellow miso
juice of 2 lemon wedges
¼ tsp chipotle powder
good dash of black pepper
1 15-oz can chickpeas,
   drained and rinsed
1 tsp cumin
½ c salsa verde
chili powder
4 tortillas

CHEF'S NOTE:
Salsa verde is a green-colored, mild salsa made from tomatillos, with jalapeños, onions, lime, cilantro, and spices.

1. Whisk the cornstarch into the water and set aside.

2. Combine chiles, nondairy milk, nutritional yeast, miso, lemon juice, chipotle powder, and black pepper in a blender and whiz until really smooth. Transfer sauce to a small saucepan, add cornstarch slurry, and bring to almost boil over medium heat, stirring regularly.

3. Once it's at a near-boil, reduce heat to low and continue stirring and cooking until it thickens a little.

4. Taste, adding more chipotle if desired (a little goes a long, long way). Set aside, away from heat.

5. Transfer chickpeas to the blender (don't worry about rinsing it out first) and pulse a few times until the chickpeas are shredded but not pureed like refried beans.

6. Transfer to a mixing bowl and combine with cumin, salsa, and several dashes of chili powder. Stir to combine. Taste, adding a little more chili powder if desired.

7. Divide bean mixture among 4 tortillas, lining it in the center of each tortilla.

8. Roll up and place the crease side down, onto a microwave-safe plate.

9. Microwave for 20 to 30 seconds, until the enchiladas are just warm and the tortillas soft. Spoon already prepared white sauce over the top and serve.

NUTRITIONAL INFORMATION 💿 **137** Calories, **1.4g** Fat, **25.6g** Carbohydrates, **4.9g** Fiber, **0g** Sugars, **5.8g** Protein *Does not include tortilla; check the nutrition label on your package.*

Bella Tacos 30 G 🥘 $

Makes 4 | This is one of my favorite quick and easy meals. These tacos come together in a flash, making it perfect for weeknight meals.

1 c water
1 tbsp low-sodium soy
  sauce
1 tbsp nutritional yeast
½ tsp Vegan
  Worcestershire Sauce
  (pg. 302)
¼ tsp garlic powder
  (granulated)
¼ tsp onion powder
  (granulated)
1 small onion, chopped
2 portobello mushrooms,
  chopped
Taco Sauce (pg. 293),
  (optional)
4 small corn tortillas
shredded lettuce
diced tomato

1. In a skillet, whisk water, low-sodium soy sauce, nutritional yeast, Worcestershire sauce, garlic powder, and onion powder together.
2. Bring to a boil over high heat.
3. Add onion and mushrooms and reduce heat to medium once boiling.
4. Continue to cook, stirring occasionally, until all liquid has evaporated.
5. Meanwhile, prepare Taco Sauce, if using.
6. Once mushrooms are cooked completely, spoon into tortillas and top with lettuce, tomato, and optional Taco Sauce.

CHEF'S NOTE: Vegemite or Marmite may be substituted for the vegan worcestershire sauce.

NUTRITIONAL INFORMATION (1 TACO, WITH TORTILLA) 🥄 **163** Calories,
1.7g Fat, **31.2g** Carbohydrates, **6g** Fiber, **2.3g** Sugars, **9.1g** Protein

Soups, Stews, & Dal

Quick Sweet Potato Soup

Serves 1 | Have a sweet potato? Then you have lunch—or dinner—in under 10 minutes!

1 c vegetable broth
2 c diced sweet potato,
   skins removed
1 garlic clove, minced
2 tsp minced fresh ginger
salt and pepper, to taste

1. Put all ingredients into a medium pot and bring to a boil.
2. Once boiling, reduce heat to low, cover, and simmer until sweet potatoes are fork-tender, about 5 minutes.
3. Pour everything into a blender and whiz until smooth, or you can leave some of it chunky.
4. Add salt and pepper to taste and serve.

CHEF'S NOTE: Add leftover cooked barley or wild rice to the soup for a fuller meal.

CHEF'S NOTE: This soup comes out a little gingery. Scale back the ginger to 1½ tsp if you want a more mellow soup and be careful when doubling the soup.

CHEF'S NOTE: If you have a high-performance blender that heats, such as a BlendTech or Vita-Mix, you can place all contents in the blender and blend until its warm (don't even bother mincing the ginger or garlic).

NUTRITIONAL INFORMATION 383 Calories, **0.9g** Fat, **87.6g** Carbohydrates, **13.9g** Fiber, **26.1g** Sugars, **8.7g** Protein

Smoked Cauliflower Soup *OKAY*

Serves 1 | I love cauliflower and I love cauliflower soup. The only problem I have is that cauliflower, although tasty, is usually pretty boring on its own. Here I've added Cajun Seasoning (pg. 277) and a hint of smoke to make cauliflower soup more flavorful and a little edgy.

1 head cauliflower,
   chopped into florets
1 c nondairy milk
½ tsp Cajun Seasoning
   (pg. 277)
¼ tsp onion powder
   (granulated)
½ tsp garlic powder
   (granulated)
dash of paprika
⅛ tsp liquid smoke
pinch of salt
juice of 1 lemon wedge
black or white pepper, to
   taste (optional)

Top with cheese
Try adding Carrots & cooked

1. Line a large pot with a thin layer of water and bring to a boil.

2. Add cauliflower, turn heat down to low, cover, and steam until cauliflower is very soft and tender, almost falling apart, about 10 minutes.

3. Meanwhile, combine nondairy milk, seasonings, a few drops of liquid smoke, salt, and lemon juice in your blender. Whiz for a few seconds so everything incorporates.

4. Add cooked cauliflower, in batches if necessary, and puree until silky and creamy, adding more nondairy milk if necessary. You want the consistency to be a thick, creamy soup or a runny gravy.

5. Pour soup into a small pot and heat gently over medium heat.

6. Taste, adding more Cajun Seasoning or liquid smoke if desired. Also add more salt, plus black or white pepper, if desired.

7. Once warm, cover and let sit for a few minutes, allowing the flavors to merge. Garnish with a dash of Cajun Seasoning.

NUTRITIONAL INFORMATION **157** Calories, **0.5g** Fat, **27.8g** Carbohydrates, **6.9g** Fiber, **19.4g** Sugars, **13.9g** Protein

Shiitake Miso Soup

Serves 1 | I often call this "feel-better soup" because it's the one soup I yearn for when I'm sick. You can also extend the servings by cleaning out your fridge. Try adding greens, leftover noodles or rice, cubed tofu, etc. I also like to add 1 teaspoon of minced fresh ginger for variety.

3 green onions
2 c water
1 c sliced shiitake
    mushrooms
tiny pinch of red pepper
    flakes
1 tbsp yellow miso
low-sodium soy sauce
    (optional)
kelp (optional)

CHEF'S NOTE:
If you use dried shiitake mushrooms, you'll need to rehydrate them in hot water first. Save the water for the broth, but be sure to strain it first to remove the grit. Approximately ½ cup of dried shiitakes equals 1 cup fresh mushrooms.

1. Cut off the rooty bottom of the green onions and discard. Then slice the white and light green parts of the green onions, and set aside.

2. Line a medium pot with a thin layer of water.

3. Add mushrooms and sauté over high heat until the mushrooms start to soften.

4. Add the red pepper flakes and 1 tablespoon of miso and cook for a few seconds, stirring to combine the miso with the water and prevent clumps.

5. Add onions and remaining water and bring to a near-boil.

6. Once soup is about to start boiling, reduce heat to low.

7. Taste, adding more miso as desired (I usually add a total of 2½ tablespoons, but all misos are different). Since some misos are less salty than others, you may need to add a splash of low-sodium soy sauce, too. If you like your miso soup to have a fish flavor (as it's traditionally served at restaurants), add kelp to taste.

8. Add any other ingredients you'd like and continue to simmer until everything is cooked and warm.

9. Turn off heat and let rest for 5 minutes, giving the flavors a chance to enhance.

NUTRITIONAL INFORMATION 🥄 **128** Calories, **1.5g** Fat, **28g** Carbohydrates, **5.2g** Fiber, **7.4g** Sugars, **5.1g** Protein

Black Bean & Salsa Soup

Serves 4 | I've been making this soup for as long as I can remember. Since it costs less than $1 per serving, it was a staple for me during college and law school when I was broke. I still love this soup, however, and make it anytime my fridge and pantry are looking pretty bare.

1 15-oz can black beans,
  drained and rinsed
1 c salsa
1½ c vegetable broth
½ tsp ground cumin
1 c frozen corn, thawed
dash of hot sauce
corn chips

1. Place 1 cup beans, salsa, broth, and cumin in a blender, and puree until smooth.
2. Transfer to a saucepan and add remaining beans, corn, and hot sauce to taste.
3. Stir to combine and heat thoroughly over low heat.
4. Once warm, serve, garnished with broken corn chips over the top. Freshly chopped cilantro and a dollop of Sour Cream (pg. 274) or vegan yogurt also make a nice garnish.

CHEF'S NOTE:
Traditional, tomato-based salsas work best in this recipe.

NUTRITIONAL INFORMATION (WITHOUT CHIPS) **133** Calories, **0.6g** Fat, **23.8g** Carbohydrates, **4.6g** Fiber, **3.2g** Sugars, **6.4g** Protein

Moroccan Lentil Soup

Serves 4 | Straight out of the pantry and into a bowl! I developed this flavorful soup a few years ago during one of my "pantry challenges." Periodically, I force myself to cook only with items found in my pantry to remind myself that a delicious and satisfying meal is always on hand, even when the fridge looks bare. (Plus it helps keep the stockpiling at bay!)

1 small onion, diced
2 garlic cloves, minced
3 c vegetable broth
½ c red lentils
1 14-oz can diced tomatoes
1 large carrot, sliced
2 celery stalks, sliced
1 tsp garam masala
1 tsp paprika
1 tsp ground ginger
½ tsp ground cumin
½ tsp ground cinnamon
½ tsp mild curry powder
salt, to taste

1. Line a medium pot with a thin layer of water and sauté onion and garlic over high heat until the water has absorbed.

2. Add remaining ingredients in order, except the salt.

3. Bring to a boil, cover, reduce heat to low, and cook for 15 minutes or until lentils are cooked (they will expand and turn orange in color).

4. Add salt to taste.

5. Transfer half of the soup to a blender and puree until smooth, then mix it back in with remaining soup (or lightly use an immersion blender).

6. Cover and leave on the warm stove for 5 to 10 minutes, allowing the flavors to merge.

NUTRITIONAL INFORMATION (1 C) 🥄 **128** Calories, **0.5g** Fat, **24.4g** Carbohydrates, **10.4g** Fiber, **5.5g** Sugars, **7.7g** Protein

Ethiopian Chickpea Stew 30 G S $

Serves 4 | I love this Ethiopian stew because it tastes like it was slowly roasted and simmered all day, but actually comes together in about 20 minutes.

1 small red onion, diced
3 garlic cloves, minced
1-inch piece fresh ginger, minced
2 to 4 tsp Berberé (pg. 275)
pinch of cardamom (optional)
1 8-oz can tomato sauce
2 c vegetable broth, divided
1 15-oz can chickpeas, drained and rinsed
½ c chickpea flour
salt and pepper, to taste

CHEF'S NOTE:
If using commercial berberé, you might want to start with 1 teaspoon. Some brands are explosive in terms of hot spices.

1. Line a large pot with a thin layer of water and sauté onion, garlic, and ginger over high heat until fragrant and onion is soft, about 2 minutes.

2. Stir in 1 to 2 teaspoons of Berberé and a pinch of cardamom, coating everything well, then add tomato sauce, 1½ cups of broth, and chickpeas.

3. Bring to a boil, cover, and simmer.

4. Meanwhile, heat a skillet. You'll know it's ready when a drop of water fizzles.

5. Add chickpea flour and, stirring constantly, continue to cook over medium heat until fragrant and toasty. The flour will turn a dark golden and then light brown. Be careful not to burn it. If you burn a little, that's fine, but you do not want a lot of dark brown or black pieces.

6. Stir the remaining ½ cup of broth (cold is best) into the toasted chickpea flour and then whisk mixture in with the soup.

7. Stir to fully incorporate and continue to cook on low for 5 minutes.

8. Taste, adding more Berberé if desired, and season with salt and pepper.

NUTRITIONAL INFORMATION ✎ **256** Calories, **3.1g** Fat, **47.6g** Carbohydrates, **10.6g** Fiber, **7.5g** Sugars, **11.4g** Protein

Cheater G-Nut Stew

Serves 4 | My friend Bethany lived in Uganda for a while and brought an amazing recipe for g-nut stew (also called Malakwang) back with her. Peanuts, which are called g-nuts (short for "ground nuts"), are used in many local dishes there and add a nice, creamy element and complex flavor. I'm calling this recipe "cheater" because it uses peanut butter (and is not fat-free) and also because it simplifies the traditional recipe.

1 c vegetable broth

1 8-oz can tomato sauce

2½ tbsp smooth peanut butter

1 15-oz can chickpeas, drained and rinsed

4 c baby spinach (or any greens you like)

1. Whisk broth and tomato sauce with peanut butter in a medium pot until well combined.

2. Heat over low heat and add chickpeas and spinach.

3. Continue to cook, stirring frequently, until thoroughly warm and spinach has cooked down.

4. Remove the stew from heat and leave to rest for 5 to 15 minutes. The longer you let it sit, the creamer the sauce will become. Letting it rest also allows the flavors to blend with the spinach and chickpeas.

CHEF'S NOTE: In Uganda, g-nut stew is traditionally served over cooked (steamed or boiled) yucca, also called cassava. Yucca is a starchy root, much like a potato, with white flesh and brown skin.

VARIATIONS

Low-Fat G-Nut Stew   Try substituting peanut flour to taste instead of peanut butter, starting with 1 tablespoon or so. Peanut flour can be found at Trader Joe's and some health food stores.

CHEF'S NOTE: You can find yucca in some supermarkets in the United States, especially Latin American and Asian grocery stores, but I actually prefer to sop up this stew with toast or Whole-Wheat Drop Biscuits (pg. 37). Coarsely mashed sweet potatoes are different, but make a decent substitute for the yucca as well.

NUTRITIONAL INFORMATION (WITH PEANUT BUTTER) 215 Calories, 6.8g Fat, 30.4g Carbohydrates, 6.8g Fiber, 3.6g Sugars, 10.6g Fat

NOLA Gumbo ③⓪ Ⓖ Ⓢ 🍲 $

Serves 4 | I was only twelve or so when my parents first took me to New Orleans. I loved everything about that city: the way the people talked, the beautiful architecture and, of course, the food. Most of the popular dishes associated with Cajun and Creole cuisine aren't normally vegetarian, but some of them, like gumbo, are often made vegetarian during Lent. This gumbo is vegan, but it captures all of the flavor Cajun cuisine is known for. The secret for great taste is making a roux, which I include here. Serve over cooked brown rice or with Bayou Cornbread (pg. 66) (break cornbread into the gumbo).

¼ c white whole-wheat flour

4 garlic cloves, minced

1 small onion, finely diced

2 celery stalks, finely diced

1 green bell pepper, seeded and diced

1 tbsp Cajun Seasoning (pg. 277)

1 to 2 tbsp Tabasco (or other hot sauce)

1 14-oz can tomatoes, undrained

1 15-oz can kidney beans, drained and rinsed

2 c vegetable broth

pinch of dried oregano

pinch of dried thyme

pinch of dried basil

1. Make sure the inside of a large pot is completely dry.

2. Toast flour over high heat, stirring frequently, until it darkens and smells toasty, taking care not to burn it.

3. Remove the flour and set aside.

4. Line the pot with a thin layer of water and sauté garlic over high heat for a minute.

5. Add onion, celery, and bell pepper, and continue to cook for 2 minutes, or until onion is translucent, the peppers are bright green, and most of the liquid has cooked off. Turn off heat and stir in flour to coat everything well.

6. Add Cajun Seasoning and hot sauce, stirring to coat; then add tomatoes with their juices, beans, and vegetable broth.

7. Add a pinch of dried oregano, thyme, and basil (use your intuition!) and stir to combine.

8. Bring to a near-boil, cover, and reduce heat to low, simmering for a few minutes until everything is warm.

9. Taste, adding more Cajun Seasoning, hot sauce (or cayenne powder) to taste, plus salt if desired.

NUTRITIONAL INFORMATION (WITHOUT RICE) 🍜 **257** Calories, **1.2g** Fat, **52.2g** Carbohydrates, **12.2g** Fiber, **8.6g** Sugars, **12.2g** Protein

CHEF'S NOTE: Gluten-free flour may be substituted for the whole-wheat.

CHEF'S NOTE: Add sliced spicy vegan sausage to this gumbo for added complexity and a more traditional flavor.

Jalapeño-Butternut Soup

Serves 2 | I'm always looking for new ways to reinvent butternut squash soup. This dish came to be one afternoon when I had nothing but butternut squash and jalapeños in my fridge, and it might be my favorite take on butternut squash soup yet!

1 c vegetable broth
1½ tbsp minced garlic
1 tbsp minced fresh
   ginger
1 tbsp minced jalapeño
1 c butternut squash, cubed
1 tbsp pure maple syrup
dash of chipotle powder
¼ tsp low-sodium soy
   sauce (optional)

1. Line a large pot with a thin layer of broth.
2. Sauté garlic, ginger, and jalapeño until fragrant, about 1 minute.
3. Add remaining broth plus butternut squash and bring to a boil.
4. Reduce heat to low and simmer until fork-tender, about 8 minutes.
5. Transfer broth and veggies to a blender, in batches if necessary, and puree until smooth and creamy, adding extra broth as necessary.
6. Return mixture to your pot and add maple syrup and chipotle powder to taste. If you make it too spicy, you can mellow it out with a little nondairy milk. Add low-sodium soy sauce to taste, or salt for a soy-free version.

CHEF'S NOTE: Sweet potatoes or yams may be substituted for the butternut squash.

NUTRITIONAL INFORMATION 76 Calories, 0.2g Fat, 18.9g Carbohydrates, 3.1g Fiber, 8.2g Sugars, 1.2g Protein

Rustic Chili 30 G ⬭ $

Serves 2 | A chili without beans? Yes! A chili without beans! Cauliflower is a great surprise ingredient in this filling and satisfying low-calorie chili.

16 oz brown mushrooms
2 c No-Beef Broth
   (pg. 298)
1 sweet onion, diced
3 garlic cloves, minced
1 15-oz can fire-roasted
   diced tomatoes
1 tbsp apple cider vinegar
2 tbsp chili powder
1 tsp ground cumin
1 tsp dried oregano
1 tbsp steak sauce (or
   ketchup)
2 tsp yellow mustard
½ tsp mild curry powder
1 head cauliflower,
   chopped into quarter-
   size florets
cayenne powder or hot
   sauce, to taste
salt and pepper, to taste

1. Pulse mushrooms in a blender or food processor until crumbled and the consistency of chopped olives.

2. Pour broth into a large pot; add mushrooms, onion, and garlic; and cook over high heat for a few minutes.

3. Add tomatoes with their juices, vinegar, and spices through curry powder, stirring to combine.

4. Add cauliflower and bring to a boil.

5. Once boiling, reduce heat to low, cover, and simmer for 10 minutes, or until cauliflower is fork-tender and golden brown in color. Be sure to stir chili occasionally to incorporate everything.

6. Taste, adding cayenne powder or hot sauce (such as Tabasco or Cholula) to taste, and season with salt and pepper.

NUTRITIONAL INFORMATION ⬭ **253** Calories, **2.9g** Fat, **46.5g** Carbohydrates, **15.1g** Fiber, **18.9g** Sugars, **18.1g** Protein

Mexican Chowder

Serves 3 | I love my chowders and I love Mexican food, so putting these two together just made sense.

1 small sweet onion,
   finely diced
2 garlic cloves, minced
1 red bell pepper, seeded
   and diced
1 green bell pepper,
   seeded and diced
2 tsp chili powder
½ tsp paprika
½ tsp ground cumin
¼ c nutritional yeast
1 c nondairy milk
2 tbsp ketchup
1 tbsp yellow miso
1 c yellow corn
1 c canned black beans
juice of 1 or more lime
   wedges
salt and pepper, to taste
corn chips (optional)
garnishes: Sour Cream
   (pg. 274), vegan yogurt,
   or chopped cilantro

1. Line a large pot with a thin layer of water and bring to a boil.
2. Add onion and garlic and sauté until onion becomes translucent, about 2 minutes.
3. Add bell peppers and spices and reduce heat to medium, continuing to cook.
4. Meanwhile, whisk ¼ cup of nutritional yeast with nondairy milk and ketchup, then pour over bell peppers, stirring to combine everything.
5. Add miso, corn, and black beans and stir in.
6. Squeeze the juice out of a lime wedge and stir.
7. Taste, adding more lime as desired plus salt and pepper to taste.
8. For a stronger cheese flavor, whisk in 1 to 2 more tbsp of nutritional yeast.
9. Serve with corn chips. You can garnish with a dollop of Sour Cream, vegan yogurt, or chopped cilantro, if desired.

CHEF'S NOTE: If your liquid is too thin, add tomato sauce, broth, or more nondairy milk.

NUTRITIONAL INFORMATION 🥄 **252** Calories, **2.4g** Fat, **43.4g** Carbohydrates, **9.6g** Fiber, **13g** Sugars, **16g** Protein

Sweet Potato Dal ③⓪ Ⓕ Ⓖ Ⓢ $

Serves 2 | *Pictured opposite and on pg. 92* | This soup is dal-icious! It's so flavorful you'll want seconds—and thirds!

1 small sweet potato,
    skinned and diced into
    ½-inch cubes
1 small onion, finely
    chopped
3 garlic cloves, minced
1 to 2 pinches red pepper
    flakes
¼ tsp turmeric
¼ tsp garam masala
1 c vegetable broth
½ c dried red lentils
4 c spinach
salt, to taste

1. Line a medium pot with a thin layer of water and sauté onion and garlic for a minute.
2. Add a pinch or two of red pepper flakes and continue to cook until all the water has cooked off.
3. Add turmeric and ¼ teaspoon of garam masala and stir to coat.
4. Add 1 cup of broth and uncooked lentils and bring to a boil.
5. Once boiling, reduce heat to low, cover, and simmer for about 5 minutes.
6. Add sweet potatoes, bring to a boil again, and reduce to low and simmer, until lentils are fully cooked (they expand and the sauce thickens), about 5 minutes more. Check periodically to see if you need additional broth (I tend to add an extra ½ cup, but it can vary).
7. Once lentils are cooked and sweet potatoes fork-tender, taste.
8. Add more garam masala as desired (I like to add another ¼ teaspoon but some blends are stronger than others).
9. Add spinach, continuing to stir until spinach cooks down and softens.
10. Season with salt to taste and serve.

NUTRITIONAL INFORMATION 🥄 **232** Calories, **0.9g** Fat, **42.2g** Carbohydrates, **17.7g** Fiber, **4.7g** Sugars, **15.4g** Protein

Salads & Dressings

Pear & Arugula Salad 30 G S O

Serves 2 | Arugula and pear were made to be together. The spiciness of arugula just goes so well with the sweetness of the pear. I've added quinoa and tart apples to this lovely union for nutritional and flavorful depth.

¼ c quinoa
½ c water
2 c arugula
1 Bosc pear, sliced
1 green apple, sliced
Balsamic-Dijon
   Vinaigrette (pg. 126)

1. Combine quinoa with ½ cup of water in a saucepan.
2. Cover and bring to a boil.
3. Once boiling, reduce heat to low and simmer until the quinoa is fluffy and water has evaporated, about 15 minutes.
4. Meanwhile plate arugula and pear and apple slices and prepare dressing.
5. Spoon cooked quinoa (warm or chilled) over salad and drizzle generously with dressing.

Make Ahead ⬤ You can make the quinoa ahead to save time, or make the entire salad, mixing all the components together (except the dressing), refrigerating and later serving as a chilled salad.

NUTRITIONAL INFORMATION ⬤ **168** Calories, **1.6g** Fat, **37.2g** Carbohydrates, **6.4g** Fiber, **16.4g** Sugars, **4.2g** Protein

Curried Quinoa Salad

Serves 2 | Curry-flavored quinoa adds a nice boost of protein to this refreshing spinach salad. It serves two as a meal or four as a side.

½ c quinoa
1 c vegetable broth
1 tsp mild yellow curry
   powder
dash of paprika
4 c fresh baby spinach
1 mango, diced
1 cucumber, sliced
2 celery stalks, sliced
   (optional)
¼ c raisins (optional)
6 oz vegan yogurt
   (optional)
fresh mint or cilantro,
   minced, to taste
   (optional)

1. Mix uncooked quinoa with broth, curry powder, and paprika in a saucepan.
2. Cover and bring to a boil.
3. Once boiling, reduce heat to low and simmer for 15 minutes, or until all the water has evaporated.
4. Toss spinach with remaining ingredients except yogurt, and plate.
5. Spoon quinoa (warm or chilled) over the top.
6. Add a dollop of plain yogurt, or the yogurt mixed with minced fresh mint or cilantro, if you want a cool dressing with the salad.

Make Ahead You can make the quinoa ahead to save time, or make the entire salad, mixing all the components together (except the yogurt), refrigerating, and later serving as a chilled salad.

CHEF'S NOTE:
For a spicy kick, sprinkle mango with chili powder before adding it to the salad.

CHEF'S NOTE: I like to leave the skin on the cucumber for added nutrition, but you can remove it.

NUTRITIONAL INFORMATION (WITHOUT YOGURT) **331** Calories, **4.1g** Fat, **66.9g** Carbohydrates, **8.01g** Fiber, **29.5g** Sugars, **12.1g** Protein

Cherry Quinoa Salad ③⓪ Ⓖ Ⓢ ⓪ $

Serves 2 | Cherries add a nice, natural sweetness to this salad so it doesn't need any dressing. It's one of my favorite light summertime meals and it's very filling. Apple slices and chopped raw walnuts also make a nice addition. This salad serves two as a meal or four as a side.

1 c water
¼ c dried cherries
½ c quinoa
4 c baby spinach
1 c chickpeas
1 cucumber, cut in half
   lengthwise, then sliced
dried cherries, for garnish
juice of 1 or more lemon
   wedges

CHEF'S NOTE:
I like to use red quinoa here so the color of the quinoa visually matches the cherry taste. However, regular (white) quinoa may be substituted.

1. Bring water to a boil.
2. Once boiling add cherries, cover, turn off heat, and let sit for 10 minutes.
3. After 10 minutes the water should take on a pink hue, some of the cherries should be floating, and all of them should look bloated.
4. Transfer to a blender and whiz until smooth (a few cherry bits are okay). Look at the markings on your blender to make sure you have 1 cup of liquid, but if not, add a little more water. if you have more than 1 cup, drain excess off.
5. Return to saucepan and add quinoa, stirring to combine.
6. Bring to a boil and once boiling, reduce heat to low and simmer until water has cooked off, about 15 minutes.
7. Meanwhile, toss spinach with remaining ingredients and plate.
8. Sprinkle with quinoa (warm or chilled) and squeeze lemon juice over the top.

Make Ahead ⬿ Soak the cherries in water overnight or all day while you're at work and skip the boiling process. You can also make the quinoa ahead to save time, or make the entire salad, mixing all the components together, refrigerating and later serving chilled.

NUTRITIONAL INFORMATION ⬿ **531** Calories, **8g** Fat, **95.1g** Carbohydrates, **20.1g** Fiber, **20.8g** Sugars, **24.3g** Protein

CHEF'S NOTE: I generally use cherry-juice-infused Craisins here since dried cherries are not available in St. Maarten, but any dried cherry that looks like a raisin (and is not the big, plump, tart variety) should work here. Pomegranate Craisins are also a good substitution.

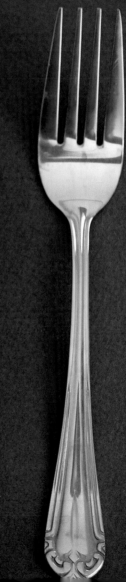

Southwest Chop Salad ③⓪ Ⓖ Ⓢ ⊝ $ ❶

Serves 1 | Pictured opposite and on pg. 116 | My all-time favorite salad and go-to lunch when it's too hot to cook.

2 c chopped lettuce
¼ c cooked brown rice
⅓ c canned black beans,
    drained and rinsed
¼ c yellow corn
¼ c chopped tomato
2 tbsp chopped cilantro
2 tbsp chopped green
    onions
corn chips (optional)

❶ Mix all ingredients together, except corn chips.

❷ Break chips over top of the salad, if using.

❸ For a dressing, use hot sauce, such as Tabasco or Cholula, with fresh lime juice or salsa. Barbecue sauce also makes a fine dressing!

CHEF'S NOTE: Cooked barley may be substituted for the brown rice.

NUTRITIONAL INFORMATION (WITHOUT DRESSING OR CORN CHIPS) ⬿
206 Calories, **1.4g** Fat, **41.3g** Carbohydrates, **7.9g** Fiber, **5.3g** Sugars, **10.1g** Protein

Strawberry & Spinach Salad

Serves 1 | This salad is absolutely stunning and has a gourmet feel about it, making it perfect for dinner parties. Plus nothing beats fresh strawberries when they're in season.

Balsamic-Dijon
  Vinaigrette (pg. 126) or
  fresh lemon juice
2 c baby spinach
1 c sliced strawberries
2 to 3 hearts of palm,
  sliced
¼ c canned white beans
  or chickpeas, or cubed
  tofu
1 tbsp chopped pecans or
  walnuts (optional)

1. Prepare dressing and set aside.
2. Plate spinach, then add remaining ingredients.
3. Drizzle dressing generously over the top and serve.

> **CHEF'S NOTE:** Thawed frozen strawberries may be substituted during the off-season, but fresh is far superior.

Balsamic-Dijon Vinaigrette

Serves 1 | This is my go-to salad dressing because it comes together in seconds. For a healthy snack, I like to dip pear slices straight into this dressing.

2 tsp Dijon mustard
1 tsp balsamic vinegar
1 tsp red wine vinegar
1 tbsp water
agave nectar, to taste

1. Whisk Dijon with vinegars and water.
2. If it's too tart, add drops of agave nectar to taste.

NUTRITIONAL INFORMATION

STRAWBERRY & SPINACH SALAD (WITHOUT DRESSING OR NUTS)
112 Calories, **1.7g** Fat, **17.4g** Carbohydrates, **6g** Fiber, **7.6g** Sugars, **10.4g** Protein

BALSAMIC-DIJON VINAIGRETTE (1 TSP) **1** Calorie, **0.1g** Fat, **0.1g** Carbohydrates, **0g** Sugars, **0g** Fiber, **0.1g** Protein

Italian Dressing ㉚ Ⓕ Ⓖ Ⓢ $ ❶

Serves 1 | While some people favor ranch, Thousand Island, or French, my pick was always Italian dressing. I like how Italian dressing brings out the subtle flavors in lettuce, tomatoes, carrots, and other salad staples, rather than masking it completely as creamy dressings tend to do. Here is my quick, go-to recipe for Italian dressing.

2 tbsp apple cider vinegar
¼ tsp Dijon mustard
Italian seasoning
dash of onion powder
    (granulated)
dash of garlic powder
    (granulated)
agave nectar, to taste

1. Whisk vinegar and Dijon mustard together.
2. Add several dashes of Italian seasoning and whisk—it should become speckled with green bits.
3. Add 2 light dashes of onion and garlic powder, and whisk again.
4. If it's too tart or acidic, add a few drops of agave nectar to taste. If it's still too sharp, add more agave nectar and try diluting it with 1 to 2 teaspoons of water or broth (some vinegars and mustards are stronger than others).

> **CHEF'S NOTE:** For a complementary salad, use romaine lettuce, tomatoes, red onions, cucumbers, and pitted black olives.

> **CHEF'S NOTE:** Feel free to try other vinegars you like here, such as distilled white vinegar or red wine vinegar.

NUTRITIONAL INFORMATION (APPROX. 3 TBSP) 🥄 **11** Calories, **0.2g** Fat, **0.9g** Carbohydrates, **0g** Fiber, **0g** Sugars, **0.1g** Protein

Deity Dressing

Makes 1 cup | This is my low-fat version of Annie's famous Goddess Dressing. It's rich and creamy and great on salads or as dipping sauce for crudités.

2 green onions
6 oz silken tofu
¼ c nondairy milk
1 small garlic clove
2 tbsp apple cider vinegar
1 tbsp fresh lemon juice
¼ tsp low-sodium soy
   sauce
⅛ tsp liquid smoke
1 to 2 tsp tahini (optional)

1. Chop the rooty bottom off the green onions.
2. Combine all ingredients in a blender and whiz until smooth and creamy.
3. Taste, adding more low-sodium soy sauce or lemon if desired.

CHEF'S NOTE: ½ package of Mori-Nu tofu (any firmness) can be substituted for the silken tofu.

Caesar Dressing

Makes 1 cup | *Pictured opposite* | This dressing makes a satisfying salad out of lettuce.

½ pkg Mori-Nu tofu
1 garlic clove
3 tbsp nondairy milk
2 tbsp nutritional yeast
1 tbsp red wine vinegar
4 tsp yellow miso
1 tsp onion powder
   (granulated)
1 tsp Dijon mustard
½ tsp Vegan
   Worcestershire Sauce
1 to 2 tsp brine from
   capers or green olives
2 to 3 tbsp fresh lemon
   juice

1. Combine all ingredients in a blender and puree until smooth.
2. Taste, adding more lemon, brine, and agave nectar if necessary.
3. If it's too thick, add another 1 tablespoon of nondairy milk.

CHEF'S NOTE: Any firmness of Mori-Nu can also be used.

NUTRITIONAL INFORMATION

DEITY DRESSING (2 TBSP, WITHOUT TAHINI) **19** Calories, **0.6g** Fat, **1.5g** Carbohydrates, **0g** Fiber, **0.8g** Sugars, **1.8g** Protein

DEITY DRESSING (2 TBSP, WITH 1 TSP TAHINI) **23** Calories, **0.9g** Fat, **1.6g** Carbohydrates, **0g** Fiber, **0.8g** Sugars, **2g** Protein

DEITY DRESSING (2 TBSP, WITH 2 TSP TAHINI) **26** Calories, **1.3g** Fat, **1.8g** Carbohydrates, **0g** Fiber, **0.8g** Sugars, **2.1g** Protein

CAESAR DRESSING (2 TBSP) **28** Calories, **0.5g** Fat, **3.2g** Carbohydrates, **0.9g** Fiber, **0.8g** Sugars, **3.3g** Protein

Thai Lettuce Wraps

Makes 6 | *Pictured opposite* | These cool and refreshing lettuce wraps make for a quick lunch, especially if you already have cooked rice on hand.

Thai Peanut Sauce
   (pg. 130), to taste
½ c cooked brown rice
1 cucumber, sliced thinly
1 c cubed tofu
1 carrot, shredded
6 lettuce leaves
3 green onions, sliced
   (optional)
bean sprouts (optional)
fresh cilantro (optional)
juice of lime wedges
   (optional)

1. Prepare the peanut sauce first and set aside so the flavors can intensify while you assemble the wraps.
2. Spoon all remaining ingredients, except lime wedges, into lettuce wraps.
3. Squeeze fresh lime juice over the top if desired.
4. Drizzle with Thai Peanut Sauce and serve.

Thai Peanut Sauce

Serves 4 | This creamy Asian-inspired peanut sauce is great as a dipping sauce or salad dressing.

1 tbsp peanut butter
1 tbsp warm water
1 tbsp sweet chili sauce
juice of 1 lime wedge
2 tsp low-sodium soy sauce
1¼ tsp rice vinegar
few light dashes of garlic
   powder (granulated)
few light dashes of
   ground ginger
1 to 2 drops Sriracha
   (Asian hot sauce)
1 tbsp nondairy milk

1. In a small microwave-safe bowl, combine peanut butter, water, chili sauce, lime juice, low-sodium soy sauce, rice vinegar, garlic powder and ground ginger, and Sriracha. If you're using unsweetened peanut butter, you might also want to include a drop or two of agave nectar.
2. Microwave for 20 seconds, whisk, then whisk in nondairy milk.
3. Taste, adding more hot sauce as desired.

NUTRITIONAL INFORMATION

THAI LETTUCE WRAPS (1 WRAP, NO SAUCE) 🍃 **82** Calories, **0.7g** Fat, **15.7g** Carbohydrates, **1.3g** Fiber, **1.6g** Sugars, **3.8g** Protein

THAI PEANUT SAUCE (1 TBSP) 🍃 **19** Calories, **1.4g** Fat, **1g** Carbohydrates, **0g** Sugars, **0g** Fiber, **0.9g** Protein

Veggie Dishes: Stir-Fries & Curries

Broccoli & Red Pepper Stir-Fry 30 G $ 1

Serves 2 | This stir-fry reminds me of the Chinese beef-and-broccoli takeout favorite, but without the beef. It comes together quickly and the sauce is to die for.

2 c water

2 tbsp low-sodium soy
   sauce

2 tbsp nutritional yeast

2 tbsp Dijon mustard

½ tsp garlic powder
   (granulated)

½ tsp onion powder
   (granulated)

½ tsp ground ginger

1 tsp Vegan Worcestershire
   Sauce (pg. 302)

1 head broccoli, chopped
   into florets

1 tsp cornstarch

1 red bell pepper, seeded
   and sliced

cooked brown rice, as
   desired

1. In a small bowl, whisk water with low-sodium soy sauce, nutritional yeast, Dijon mustard, spices and Vegan Worcestershire Sauce.

2. Pour half into a skillet and bring to a boil.

3. Add broccoli and cook over high heat for a few minutes, until the broccoli turns bright green and the sauce has mostly cooked off.

4. Whisk cornstarch into remaining broth until well combined and then pour over broccoli.

5. Add bell peppers and continue to cook over high heat until the broccoli is dark green, the bell peppers are tender but still crisp, and the sauce has reduced down but is not completely evaporated (you want a good bit of sauce).

6. Spoon broccoli and bell pepper over cooked brown rice and drizzle with remaining sauce.

NUTRITIONAL INFORMATION (WITHOUT RICE) **189** Calories, **2.5g** Fat, **33.1g** Carbohydrates, **12.5g** Fiber, **8.5g** Sugars, **15.8g** Protein

Ginger-Miso Quinoa Stir-Fry 30 G

Serves 2 | Bringing quinoa into this stir-fry adds a nice serving of protein and also cuts the total cook time in half.

½ c quinoa
1 c water
1 c vegetable broth
1 tbsp yellow miso
2-inch piece fresh ginger, minced, divided
1 tbsp rice vinegar
1 tsp low-sodium soy sauce
pinch of red pepper flakes
a few drops of agave nectar
8 oz shiitake mushrooms, sliced (optional)
1 red bell pepper, seeded and sliced
6 oz snap peas
2 baby bok choy, chopped

CHEF'S NOTE:
For presentation place a small mound of cooked quinoa on two plates, then add stir-fry veggies on top and drizzle with remaining cooking liquid.

1. In a small pot, combine uncooked quinoa with water, cover, and bring to a boil. Once boiling, reduce heat to low and continue to cook until water has been absorbed and quinoa is cooked, about 15 minutes.

2. Meanwhile, line a large skillet or pot with a thin layer of broth. Add miso, half of the ginger, rice vinegar, low-sodium soy sauce, red pepper flakes, and a few drops of agave nectar; whisk to combine.

3. Cook over high heat for a minute or two, until ginger is fragrant and sauce is boiling. Add mushrooms and cook for another minute.

4. Add remaining broth and bell pepper and continue to cook until bell peppers start to soften, about 3 minutes. Add remaining ginger and snap peas, stirring to combine.

5. Reduce heat to medium, add bok choy, and cover.

6. Continue to cook for a few minutes, then stir again. Keep cooking until bell peppers and bok choy are cooked, but still crisp (think al dente).

7. Meanwhile, taste sauce, adding a dab more miso or low-sodium soy sauce if necessary (some miso brands are saltier than others).

NUTRITIONAL INFORMATION ⟵ **357** Calories, **4.7g** Fat, **63.9g** Carbohydrates, **11.9g** Fiber, **12.5g** Sugars, **16.7g** Protein

Pineapple Tempeh Teriyaki Stir-Fry

Serves 3 | Pineapple juice gives this tempeh teriyaki stir-fry a bit of an island or Hawaiian feel to it.

1 8-oz pkg tempeh
¼ c teriyaki sauce
1 c pineapple juice
1 onion, sliced
1 green bell pepper,
   seeded and sliced
1 red bell pepper, seeded
   and sliced
1 tbsp cornstarch
1 tbsp low-sodium soy
   sauce
cooked brown rice, as
   desired
crushed pineapple
   (optional)

CHEF'S NOTE:
Adding a little ginger really makes the pineapple sparkle in this dish. You can add ground ginger to the marinade or sprinkle it over top.

1. Cut tempeh into slices roughly the size of your finger.

2. Mix teriyaki sauce with pineapple juice and marinate tempeh overnight or for several hours (putting it together before work, for instance).

3. Line a skillet with a thin layer of water and sauté onion and peppers over high heat until onion is soft and translucent and peppers are al dente (just barely softened). Transfer to a plate or bowl and set aside.

4. Add tempeh plus a little of the marinade to line the skillet and cook over medium heat until the tempeh pieces are warm and most of the liquid has cooked off, about 3 minutes.

5. Meanwhile, whisk cornstarch with the remaining marinade.

6. Once tempeh is warm, pour marinade over the top, stirring to combine.

7. Raise heat to high and let the sauce thicken, stirring occasionally for a minute or two.

8. Taste. If it's too sweet, add 1 tablespoon of low-sodium soy sauce, or to taste.

9. Stir to combine again, then stir in peppers and onion.

10. Serve over brown rice, and, if desired, garnish generously with crushed pineapple.

NUTRITIONAL INFORMATION (WITHOUT RICE) **264** Calories, **8.5g** Fat, **32.6g** Carbohydrates, **2.5g** Fiber, **16.7g** Sugars, **17.3g** Protein

Ginger Bok Choy Stir-Fry

Serves 2 | Living in the Caribbean has really turned me on to cooking with—and eating!—fresh ginger. Here I've paired it with baby bok choy, one of my favorite vegetables and one of the most underutilized. Serve this dish over cooked quinoa, whole-wheat couscous, or brown rice. You can also toss in a few shelled edamame (soybeans) for a boost of protein.

1 bunch green onions, sliced in half

2 baby bok choy, quartered

1 red bell pepper, seeded and sliced

1 cup vegetable broth, divided

3 garlic cloves, minced

pinch of red pepper flakes

1 tbsp low-sodium soy sauce

3 tsp minced fresh ginger

1. Cut the dark green parts and root end off the green onions, slicing the remaining white and light green parts in half lengthwise. Chop the bottom off the bok choy, then quarter it lengthwise. Set aside onions and bok choy aside with sliced red pepper.

2. Pour ⅓ cup of the vegetable broth into a large skillet.

3. Add garlic, pinch of red pepper flakes, and low-sodium soy sauce.

4. Bring to a boil over high heat and sauté garlic for 2 minutes.

5. Add green onions and cook for another minute, then add another ⅓ cup of broth and ginger, and cook another minute or two.

6. Add bell peppers, bok choy, and remaining broth.

7. Turn heat to medium and continue to cook until veggies are cooked but still fairly crisp, then serve.

- TRY 2 tsp ginger
- Make sure only a pinch of red pepper!
- use/find the baby bok choy! adult bok choy too harsh

NUTRITIONAL INFORMATION 106 Calories, **1.3g** Fat, **19.6g** Carbohydrates, **7g** Fiber, **5.6g** Sugars, **8.7g** Protein

Bell Pepper Stir-Fry 30 F G $ 1

Serves 2 | I really love bell peppers, especially in a stir-fry. They immediately improve the presentation with their beautiful color, and their delicate flavor always adds a sweet complexity. However, it's the sauce in this dish that's the real star. For a complete meal, add 1 cup adzuki beans or cubed tofu.

3 garlic cloves, minced
1 shallot, finely diced
1-inch piece fresh ginger, minced
2 tbsp low-sodium soy sauce
¼ tsp ground coriander
¼ tsp ground cumin
pinch of red pepper flakes
3 bell peppers, seeded and sliced
cooked brown rice, as desired

1. Line a skillet with ½ cup of water.
2. Sauté garlic, shallot, and ginger over high heat for a minute, then stir in low-sodium soy sauce and spices.
3. Add bell peppers and continue to cook until peppers are fork-tender but still crisp (al dente), adding more water as necessary. (You want a sauce to line the skillet).
4. Serve over warm brown rice.

CHEF'S NOTE: 2 to 3 tablespoons finely diced red onion can be used in place of the shallot.

NUTRITIONAL INFORMATION (WITHOUT RICE) 👁 **87** Calories, **0.8g** Fat, **17g** Carbohydrates, **4.6g** Fiber, **8.6g** Sugars, **3.5g** Protein

Spicy Mushroom Stir-Fry 30 Ⓖ ⬭ $

Serves 2 | *Pictured opposite and on pg 132* | I don't know what it is about white mushrooms, but I can't pass them up in the grocery store even when I know I have some on hand already. Since mushrooms tend to accent my recipes rather than star in them, I decided to create this stir-fry that focuses on the mushrooms and their unique texture. For a complete meal, add edamame or cubed tofu.

1 c vegetable broth, divided

2 tbsp low-sodium soy sauce

1 tsp rice vinegar

1 to 2 tbsp sweet red chili sauce

pinch of red pepper flakes (optional)

1-in piece ginger, minced

3 garlic cloves, minced

8 oz white mushrooms, sliced

1 red bell pepper, seeded and sliced

8 oz snap peas

cooked brown rice, as desired

1. Line a skillet with a thin layer of broth and stir in low-sodium soy sauce, rice vinegar, red chili sauce, and optional red pepper flakes.

2. Add ginger and garlic and sauté until fragrant, about 1 minute.

3. Add mushrooms and sauté until they start to soften, another minute or so.

4. Add bell pepper and snap peas and continue to sauté until al dente (cooked but still crisp), adding remaining broth halfway through.

5. Serve over rice or tossed with noodles.

NUTRITIONAL INFORMATION (WITHOUT RICE) 👈 **97** Calories, **0.7g** Fat, **16.9g** Carbohydrates, **5.5g** Fiber, **7.3g** Sugars, **7g** Protein

Sweet & Sour Tempeh

Serves 4 | Chinese take-in! Serve this classic dish over brown rice with broccoli or a mixture of bell peppers, onions, carrots, and pineapple cooked in additional sauce for that real Chinese takeout feel.

1 8-oz pkg tempeh
2 tbsp rice vinegar
2 tbsp low-sodium soy
   sauce
2 tbsp ketchup
½ tsp ground ginger
agave nectar, to taste
1 tsp cornstarch
½ c water
hot sauce, to taste

1. Cut tempeh into thin, short strips, but not so thin they break and fall apart easily. (It's better to be too thick than too thin.) This should yield about 13 slices; set aside.

2. In a small bowl or measuring cup, whisk rice vinegar, low-sodium soy sauce, ketchup, and ginger together.

3. Taste, adding a few drops of agave nectar as desired for a sweeter sauce.

4. Whisk in cornstarch and water and set aside.

5. Line a large skillet with a thin layer of water and a splash of hot sauce. Bring to a boil.

6. Once boiling, add tempeh, trying not to overlap if possible and continue cooking, flipping tempeh strips over a few times, until most (but not all) of the liquid has cooked off.

7. Reduce heat to medium and add sauce over the top.

8. Continue to cook, flipping pieces gently to ensure they are evenly coated, until the sauce reduces and thickens into a loose glaze (not to the point where it's a gloopy Jell-O).

CHEF'S NOTE: I really like to use veggie tempeh here, as opposed to plain "soy" tempeh.

NUTRITIONAL INFORMATION (4 STRIPS) 129 Calories, 6.1g Fat, 8.6g Carbohydrates, 1.9g Sugars, 2.5g Fiber, 11.2g Protein

Cauliflower-Pumpkin Curry

Serves 2 | This curry is so quick to make and an excellent use for leftover canned pumpkin. For a complete meal, serve over cooked brown rice and add in some chickpeas or cubed tofu for a bit of protein.

1 head cauliflower,
  chopped into florets
¾ c canned pure pumpkin
¾ c vegetable broth
2 tsp mild curry powder
½ tsp ground cumin
¼ tsp ground ginger
light dash of paprika
pinch of salt

1. Steam cauliflower florets until just fork-tender.

2. In a small saucepan, whisk pumpkin with broth, 2 teaspoons of curry powder, cumin, ginger, paprika, and salt.

3. Gently warm over low heat and taste, adding more curry powder if desired. (I find some curries are hotter and more potent than others.)

4. Add more salt to taste, if necessary, and toss sauce with cooked cauliflower until the florets are well coated.

CHEF'S NOTE:
For a rustic texture and nutty flavor, roast cauliflower for 35 to 40 minutes at 420°F instead of steaming.

CHEF'S NOTE: You can add smooth peanut butter or, for a low-fat option, peanut flour, to taste, 1 teaspoon at a time, to make Peanut Pumpkin Curry.

CHEF'S NOTE: A light dash of cinnamon or pumpkin pie spice helps bring out the pumpkin flavor if you want it extra "pumpkin-y."

NUTRITIONAL INFORMATION 🥄 88 Calories, **1.3g** Fat, **16.3g** Carbohydrates, **6.7g** Fiber, **6.5g** Sugars, **5.8g** Protein

Gobi Palak Ⓖ Ⓢ ⊜ Ⓢ

Serves 2 | Gobi Palak translates as "cauliflower spinach," which is exactly what this dish is. It's a delicious yellow split-pea-and-spinach dish with cauliflower that presents beautifully and requires very little effort to pull together. For a fuller meal, pair with cooked brown rice, whole-wheat roti, or naan.

3 c vegetable broth, divided
1 tbsp ketchup
pinch of red pepper flakes
1 c dried yellow split peas
1 tsp garam masala
½ tsp turmeric
½ tsp ground cumin
¼ tsp ground ginger
1 tsp prepared yellow mustard
2 c cauliflower florets
4 c baby spinach
salt and pepper, to taste

CHEF'S NOTE:
Fresh or frozen cauliflower florets may be used.

1. In a large pot, combine 2 cups of broth with ketchup and red pepper flakes and bring to a boil on high heat. Add uncooked split peas, cover, and bring to a boil again.

2. Once boiling, reduce the heat to low and simmer for 45 minutes to 1 hour, or until most of the liquid has evaporated and the split peas are softer, but not mushy (al dente).

3. Mix in the remaining spices and mustard, stirring to combine, then add the cauliflower and remaining 1 cup of broth. Cover, turn the heat to high again, and bring to a boil.

4. Reduce heat to low and continue to cook, stirring occasionally to make sure the cauliflower gets coated with the cooking liquid (the cauliflower should turn yellow).

5. Once the cauliflower is fork-tender, but not mushy or falling apart, turn the heat off completely and add the spinach, using a spatula to gently stir and incorporate. After a few strokes, the spinach will start to wilt and turn a deeper green. Continue to stir until it has cooked down and is fully incorporated.

6. Cover and let rest for a few minutes to allow the flavors to merge. Season with salt and pepper.

NUTRITIONAL INFORMATION 🥄 **446** Calories, **3.8g** Fat, **71.2g** Carbohydrates, **29.3g** Fiber, **13.3g** Sugars, **35.6g** Protein

Chana Saag ㉚ Ⓕ Ⓖ Ⓢ ⬜ Ⓢ

Serves 2 | Saag is a traditional North Indian spinach dish that is usually served as a side. Here I've made saag into a meal on its own by pairing it with hearty chickpeas (chana). For a complete meal, serve with cooked brown rice, whole-wheat roti, or naan.

1 small onion, diced
4 garlic cloves, minced
1-inch piece fresh ginger,
    minced
¼ c tomato sauce
1 tsp ground coriander
½ tsp ground cumin
1 tsp garam masala
¼ tsp turmeric
⅛ tsp ground cardamom
    (optional)
1 15-oz can chickpeas,
    drained and rinsed
¾ tsp mild yellow curry
    powder
6 c baby spinach, rinsed
salt and pepper, to taste
Tofu Yogurt
    (optional; pg. 20)

1. Line a large pot with a thin layer of water and bring to a boil.
2. Add onion, garlic, and fresh ginger.
3. Continue to cook over high heat until onion starts to become translucent, about 3 minutes.
4. Add tomato sauce, coriander, cumin, garam masala, turmeric, and cardamom, if using.
5. Stir to coat the onion mixture. Add a splash of water if necessary—you want there to always be a good bit of sauce.
6. Add chickpeas and mix again.
7. Reduce heat to low and cook, stirring to coat the chickpeas, for a minute or so.
8. Mix in curry powder, stirring to combine.
9. Add another splash of water, if necessary, and spinach. Stir the spinach around until it turns dark green and wilty.
10. Add salt and pepper to taste and serve with a dollop of Tofu Yogurt, if desired.

CHEF'S NOTE:
Like heat? Add
cayenne with
initial spices.

CHEF'S NOTE: 2 teaspoons of ground ginger
may be substituted for fresh. Add with other spices
during cooking.

NUTRITIONAL INFORMATION (WITHOUT YOGURT) 🥄 **493** Calories, **0.4g** Fat,
15.9g Carbohydrates, **1.9g** Fiber; **9.6g** Sugars, **2.5g** Protein

Casseroles & Rice Dishes

Greens Quiche

Serves 6 | I developed this recipe to save a bunch of greens that were languishing in my fridge. It'll work with any leafy greens you have on hand, particularly sturdy greens like kale, chard, and collards, and although it's crustless, it firms up nicely so you can cut perfect pieces. Who knew wilty leftovers could taste so good?

1 lb extra-firm tofu
¼ c nutritional yeast
¼ c cornstarch
1½ tbsp Dijon mustard
1 tbsp lemon juice
1 tsp onion powder
    (granulated)
1 tsp garlic powder
    (granulated)
½ tsp turmeric
½ tsp salt
¼ tsp red pepper flakes
4 c chopped greens

1. Preheat oven to 350°F.

2. Grease a shallow 9-inch pie dish and set aside.

3. Combine all ingredients, except greens, in a food processor or blender and whiz until smooth and creamy, stopping to break up chunks and scrape the sides as necessary.

4. Mix in greens and transfer batter to a pie dish.

5. Using a spatula, spread the mixture around so it's even and tight.

6. Bake for 30 to 40 minutes, or until golden and the center is firm (not mushy).

7. Allow to cool for at least 10 minutes before slicing (room temp is best).

Make Ahead ✎ You can make and store the mixture in an airtight container until you're ready to bake, or bake the quiche a day or two ahead of time and gently reheat it in your oven on warm for 10 to 20 minutes.

NUTRITIONAL INFORMATION ✎ **84** Calories, **1.2g** Fat, **10.7g** Carbohydrates, **2.4g** Fiber, **0.8g** Sugars, **9.2g** Protein

Cajun Cornbread Casserole

Serves 4 | Any excuse to eat cornbread at dinner is a good one in my book. This delicious and spicy cornbread-topped casserole is a complete meal with grains, beans, and vegetables all in one dish. Serve with hot sauce, such as Tabasco, on the table.

1 15-oz can diced tomatoes, undrained

1 small onion, diced

2 celery stalks, minced

3 garlic cloves, minced

1 bell pepper, seeded and diced

2 tbsp Cajun Seasoning (pg. 277)

1 15-oz can kidney beans, drained and rinsed

1 c cornmeal

1½ tsp baking powder

pinch of salt

1 to 2 tbsp raw sugar (optional)

¾ c nondairy milk

¼ c unsweetened applesauce

> **CHEF'S NOTE:**
> Any bell pepper will work here, but green bell peppers are more authentic.

1. Preheat oven to 400°F. Grease an 8- or 9-inch square baking pan or casserole dish.

2. Drain tomato juices into a skillet and chop tomatoes into smaller pieces; set aside.

3. Add water as necessary until a thin layer of liquid covers the skillet.

4. Sauté onion, celery, garlic, and bell pepper over high heat until onion is translucent, bell pepper slices are tender, and all of the water has evaporated, about 4 minutes.

5. Turn off heat and mix in 1 to 2 tablespoons of Cajun Seasoning, tomatoes, and kidney beans, stirring to combine, and set side.

6. In a small mixing bowl, whisk cornmeal, baking powder, salt, and additional Cajun Seasoning if desired (several dashes so the flour looks speckled when stirred). You can also add 1 to 2 tablespoons of sugar for a sweet cornbread topping. Then stir in nondairy milk and applesauce. It should be thick, but spreadable like hummus, and not dry.

7. Pour bean mixture into your baking dish and pat down firmly with a spatula. Spread cornbread mixture on top and bake for 30 to 35 minutes, or until the cornbread is a deep golden, cracked and firm to the touch. Let set out for 15 minutes before serving.

NUTRITIONAL INFORMATION 〜 **269** Calories, **1.9g** Fat, **54.3g** Carbohydrates, **10.9g** Fiber, **11.1g** Sugars, **11.6g** Protein

Tex-Mex Shepherd's Pie

Serves 4 | Shepherd's pie gets a colorful makeover complete with Tex-Mex flavorings.

1 14-oz can fire-roasted
　diced tomatoes
2 garlic cloves, minced
1 small sweet onion, diced
1 green bell pepper,
　seeded and diced
1 tsp chili powder
½ tsp ground cumin
½ tsp dried oregano
salt and pepper
1 11-oz can corn, drained
1 15-oz can black beans,
　drained and rinsed
3 sweet potatoes, cooked
　and mashed
hot sauce (optional)

1. Drain juice from tomatoes straight into a large skillet. Add a splash of water if needed so enough liquid lines the bottom of the skillet.

2. Add garlic, onion, and bell pepper and sauté over high heat until green pepper starts to get tender, about 3 minutes.

3. Add chili powder, cumin, oregano, a pinch of salt, a few dashes of black pepper, and stir to coat.

4. Taste. If you'd like a hotter flavor, add some hot sauce or more chili powder.

5. Add corn and black beans and stir to combine everything.

6. Continue to cook over medium until everything is thoroughly warm.

7. Spoon into a casserole or baking dish, and then spread mashed sweet potatoes on top (no baking necessary).

8. Serve with hot sauce on the table.

CHEF'S NOTE:
This casserole is also great as a dip: serve with baked corn chips at a party.

CHEF'S NOTE: To make mashed sweet potatoes, skin and boil the potatoes. Beat with an electric mixer, adding splashes of nondairy milk as you go. Sweet potatoes generally require more liquid than regular potatoes when beating. Once you get the right consistency, add salt and pepper to taste, plus a dash of chili powder.

NUTRITIONAL INFORMATION 🥄 **319** Calories, **1.2g** Fat, **67.5g** Carbohydrates, **11.4g** Fiber, **8.2g** Sugars, **9.4g** Protein

Fiesta Bake Ⓖ Ⓢ $

Serves 4 | If you think pasta casseroles are lame, think again. This pasta casserole is where it's at. It totally brings "Mexican" to "mac 'n' cheese." You want to use a traditional, tomato-based salsa here, mild or hot—your choice.

½ lb whole-wheat pasta

1 11-oz can corn, drained and rinsed

1 15-oz can black beans, drained and rinsed

1 4-oz can diced green chilies, drained (optional)

1¼ c nondairy milk

⅓ c nutritional yeast

2 tbsp yellow miso

2 tbsp cornstarch

1 tsp onion powder (granulated)

1 tsp garlic powder (granulated)

½ tsp paprika

¼ tsp turmeric

1 c salsa

1 tomato, sliced (optional)

fresh cilantro for garnish

1. Preheat oven to 350°F.

2. Cook pasta according to package directions and immediately rinse under cold water.

3. Meanwhile, or afterward to reduce cleanup (by using same pot), make the cheese sauce by whisking nondairy milk through turmeric together in a saucepan. Heat over medium heat until it thickens. Add salsa to cheese sauce, starting with 1 cup. If your salsa is really chunky, add another ¼ to ½ cup of salsa, but if the salsa is watery, do not.

4. Mix prepared cheese sauce with pasta, beans, and corn together.

5. Pour mixture into a casserole dish and bake for 15 to 25 minutes, or until a crisp outer crust starts to form and the casserole is totally warm.

6. Garnish with chopped cilantro and tomato slices if desired.

> **CHEF'S NOTE:** To make this dish gluten-free use brown-rice pasta; to keep it soy-free, use a soy-free miso, such as miso made from chickpeas.

NUTRITIONAL INFORMATION (WITH CHEDDAR CHEESY SAUCE) 🍈
486 Calories, **3.7g** Fat, **90.6g** Carbohydrates, **14.1g** Fiber, **11.2g** Sugars, **24.2g** Protein

Veggie Biscuit Potpie

Serves 2 | Down-home cookin'! I actually made this recipe on camera for the *Huffington Post* after one of their reporters mentioned that watching *True Blood* made her want to eat vegan. Well, this potpie is for you, Sookie Stackhouse!

Whole-Wheat Drop
    Biscuits (pg. 37)
1 c vegetable or
    No-Chicken Broth
    Powder (pg. 299)
2 tbsp cornstarch
1 c nondairy milk
2 tsp Poultry Seasoning
    Mix (pg. 276)
2½ c mixed frozen
    vegetables
2 tbsp nutritional yeast
½ tsp onion powder
    (granulated)
½ tsp garlic powder
    (granulated)

1. Prepare and bake biscuits.
2. While biscuits are baking, whisk cornstarch and broth together until well combined.
3. Then combine all ingredients (except biscuits) in a saucepan and bring to a boil over medium heat. Allow sauce to thicken as desired.
4. Taste, adding more garlic, onion, salt, or pepper to taste.
5. Pour over cooked biscuits and serve.

CHEF'S NOTE:
A pinch of dried parsley makes this gravy pretty!

NUTRITIONAL INFORMATION (WITHOUT BISCUITS) **186** calories, **1.3g** Fat, **34.1g** Carbohydrates, **6.4g** Fiber, **11.2g** Sugars, **12.4g** Protein

Dijon Rice with Broccoli

Serves 2 | Dijon mustard and broccoli complement each other beautifully and come together to jazz up a side of rice. Since all Dijon mustards and hot sauces are a little different, this recipe is very much "to taste."

1 c cooked brown rice
2 c broccoli florets, fresh
   or frozen
2 to 3 tsp Dijon mustard
1½ tsp low-sodium soy
   sauce
¼ to ½ tsp hot sauce
agave nectar or sugar to
   taste (optional)

1. Steam broccoli or, if frozen, microwave as directed.

2. Meanwhile, whisk 2 teaspoons of Dijon mustard, low-sodium soy sauce, and hot sauce together.

3. Taste, adding more hot sauce and Dijon mustard if needed. (I usually add up to 1½ teaspoons of hot sauce and 3 to 4 teaspoons of Dijon). If the Dijon is too strong for your liking, add a few drops of agave nectar or a pinch of sugar to help cut it.

4. Mix with cooked rice (if using leftover rice, add a splash of broth or water before reheating it).

5. Then mix in cooked broccoli, season with salt and pepper, and serve.

CHEF'S NOTE: Broccoli rabe also works well in this dish.

NUTRITIONAL INFORMATION 🐟 **150** Calories, **1.4g** Fat, **30.6g** Carbohydrates, **3.6g** Fiber, **1.7g** Sugars, **5.3g** Protein

Arroz Amarillo Ⓖ Ⓢ 🍲 🍱 Ⓢ

Serves 3 | Pictured opposite and on pg. 150 | Arroz Amarillo, which translates to "yellow rice," is a flavorful side dish in Cuban cuisine. Here I've paired it with peas (as it's traditionally served) and black beans to make it into a full meal.

½ c brown rice
1 c vegetable broth
1 tsp onion powder
   (granulated)
1 tsp garlic powder
   (granulated)
½ tsp turmeric
¼ tsp ground cumin
⅛ tsp paprika
dash of ground ginger
10 oz frozen peas
2 c canned black beans,
   drained and rinsed
diced tomato for garnish
   (optional)
sliced green onion for
   garnish (optional)

❶ In a medium pot, combine uncooked rice with broth and spices, stirring to combine.

❷ Cover and bring to a boil.

❸ Once boiling, reduce heat to low and simmer for 45 minutes, or until rice is cooked and all liquid has absorbed.

❹ Cook peas according to package instructions (microwave is quickest) and mix into rice.

❺ Serve alongside black beans, or mix the beans into the rice with the peas.

❻ Garnish with diced tomato and sliced green onion, if desired.

Make Ahead 🥄 The rice or the entire dish can be made in advance, with an added reward: this rice gets more flavorful the next day. If the rice is looking dry, add a little water or vegetable broth to it when you reheat.

NUTRITIONAL INFORMATION 🥄 **323** Calories, **1.9g** Fat, **62.1g** Carbohydrates, **10.7g** Fiber, **4.1g** Sugars, **14.2g** Protein

Caribbean Peas & Rice Ⓖ Ⓢ ◯ Ⓢ

Serves 4 | Peas and rice, a popular dish in the Caribbean, is traditionally made with pigeon peas, which are a legume, but circular-shaped like a green pea. In my interpretation, I substituted black-eyed peas, which are more common, and I also added a little Creole flair to complement the change. Serve with jalapeño hot sauce on the table.

2½ cups vegetable broth, divided

1 bunch green onions

2 celery stalks, minced

4 garlic cloves, minced

1 tbsp minced fresh ginger

4 fresh thyme twigs

1½ tsp Tabasco Green Jalapeño Pepper Sauce

2 tsp jerk seasoning, divided

1 cup brown rice

2 tbsp ketchup

½ tsp turmeric

1 bunch kale

1 15-oz can black-eyed peas, drained and rinsed

CHEF'S NOTE:
Chard and other leafy greens make a fine substitution for kale.

1. Thinly slice the white parts of the green onions, saving darker green parts for another use or for garnish, then set aside.

2. Line a large pot with a thin layer of broth and add green onions, celery, garlic, ginger, thyme, jalapeño sauce, and 1 teaspoon of jerk seasoning.

3. Cook over high heat, adding additional broth as necessary, until the celery is soft, about 3 minutes.

4. Add remaining jerk seasoning, stirring to coat.

5. Stir in rice with 2 cups of vegetable broth, then add 2 squirts (about 2 tablespoons) of ketchup and turmeric (for color), stirring to combine.

6. Cover and bring to a boil.

7. Once boiling, reduce heat to low and simmer for 40 to 50 minutes, until rice is cooked, but keep an eye on it, as you may need to add more broth or water during cooking (some brown rice is very thirsty).

8. Meanwhile, pull kale leaves away from the stem and chop or tear leaves into bite-sized pieces.

9. Lightly steam or cook greens, taking care to press out any excess water. (See cooking method on pg. 191.)

10. Once rice is fully cooked, fluff with a spatula then stir in greens and black-eyed peas. Salt to taste.

NUTRITIONAL INFORMATION ⬱ **322** Calories, **3.7g** Fat, **63.3g** Carbohydrates, **5g** Fiber, **3g** Sugars, **14.9g** Protein

CHEF'S NOTE: Peas and rice is commonly served with sliced pork sausage. You can use any homemade or commercial vegan sausage here; just be sure to cut the links on a diagonal for a nice presentation.

Mardi Gras Beans & Rice Ⓖ Ⓢ Ⓢ

Serves 2 | They'll make you wanna get up and scream "hallelujah!"

1 14-oz can diced fire-
    roasted tomatoes
1 c brown rice
2 c vegetable broth
1 small onion, minced
2 celery stalks, minced
1 tsp Cajun Seasoning
    (pg. 277)
1 15-oz can kidney beans,
    drained and rinsed
agave nectar or sugar, to
    taste (optional)

1. Drain juices from tomatoes into a small pot, then add uncooked rice and vegetable broth.
2. Bring to a boil, cover and reduce heat to low, and simmer until rice is fully cooked, about 40 to 45 minutes.
3. Meanwhile, line a skillet with a thin layer of water and sauté onion and celery for a minute or so, until onion is translucent.
4. Add Cajun Seasoning, stirring to combine, and turn off heat.
5. Puree half of the diced tomatoes in a blender or food processor until completely smooth like tomato sauce.
6. Pour into onion and celery mixture, stirring to combine.
7. Turn heat back on to medium and cook for a few minutes.
8. Taste. If it's too acidic, add a drop or two of agave nectar or a bit of sugar to cut the acid. You can also add more Cajun Seasoning if desired.
9. Add tomatoes and kidney beans, and stir to combine.
10. Cover and keep on low, stirring occasionally.
11. Once the rice is done, plate it and spoon the bean-tomato mixture over top.
12. Serve with hot sauce, such as Tabasco or Cholula.

NUTRITIONAL INFORMATION 🐟 **608** Calories, **3.9g** Fat, **123.9g** Carbohydrates, **22.9g** Fiber, **7.5g** Sugars, **21.8g** Protein

Teriyaki Rice

Serves 2 | So simple and yet so delicious. I enjoy the taste of plain brown rice but get bored of it easily. A little teriyaki and hot sauce completely transforms the rice into a quick and flavorful side dish.

1 c cooked brown rice
1 tbsp teriyaki sauce
hot sauce, to taste
   (optional)

1. Mix brown rice with teriyaki sauce, adding more sauce if necessary or desired. The rice should have a light coating, but shouldn't be wet. Add hot sauce if desired and serve.

Curried Rice

Serves 4 | *Pictured opposite* | Living in the Caribbean turned me on to cooking with curry seasonings. This rice is stunning when it's served, especially if you add peas for added color.

1 c brown rice
2 c vegetable broth
1 tbsp mild curry powder
1 tsp onion powder
   (granulated)
½ tsp chili powder
¼ tsp ground cumin
dash of paprika, ground
   cinnamon, and tumeric
¼ c tomato sauce

1. Combine all ingredients except tomato sauce and cayenne in a medium pot and bring to a boil.

2. Once boiling, reduce heat to low and simmer for 45 minutes, or until the rice is cooked: fluffy with no water remaining.

3. While rice is still hot, stir in the tomato sauce and coat completely.

4. Add cayenne or hot sauce (optional, if desired) to taste and season with salt and pepper.

NUTRITIONAL INFORMATION

TERIYAKI RICE 🍃 **117** Calories, **0.8g** Fat, **24.3g** Carbohydrates, **1.8g** Fiber, **1.3g** Sugars, **2.8g** Protein

CURRIED RICE (½ C) 🍃 **183** Calories, **1.6g** Fat, **38.3g** Carbohydrates, **2.6g** Fiber, **0.7g** Sugars, **4g** Protein

Beans & Faux Meat

Moroccan Sweet Potatoes & Chickpeas

Serves 2 | True to the sweet-savory flavoring Moroccan cuisine is known for, this easy dish showcases Moroccan flavors using pantry staples, for a quick and satisfying meal. For a complete meal, serve over cooked greens.

1 tsp ground coriander
1 tsp ground cumin
½ tsp paprika
¼ tsp ground cinnamon
¾ tsp ground ginger
3 sweet potatoes, skinned and diced
1 15-oz can chickpeas, drained and rinsed
juice of 1 lemon
lemon wedges for garnish

CHEF'S NOTE: Diced butternut squash is a fine substitution when it's in season, though the bake time may be longer, roughly 30 to 45 minutes. Bake squash by itself first, then add chickpeas toward the end of the baking cycle.

1. Preheat oven to 375°F. Line a large cookie sheet with parchment paper and set aside.

2. Mix the spices together in a small bowl, whisking to combine, and set aside.

3. Rinse sweet potatoes under cold water and transfer to a large mixing bowl.

4. Pour half the spice mixture over the top and mix with your hands until well coated.

5. Transfer sweet potatoes to a cookie sheet, making sure there is no overlap, and set aside.

6. Rinse chickpeas under cold water, then transfer to the mixing bowl and cover with remaining spices.

7. Mix with your hands until well combined and transfer to the cookie sheet.

8. Bake sweet potatoes and chickpeas for 10 to 15 minutes, or until sweet potatoes are fork-tender.

9. Halfway through, give the chickpeas a good shake so they turn over. You want the chickpeas to be golden and slightly crisp.

10. Squeeze lemon over sweet potatoes and chickpeas before serving. Serve over cooked greens with additional lemon wedges.

NUTRITIONAL INFORMATION 🥄 **532** Calories, **3.2g** Fat, **111.7g** Carbohydrates, **19.8g** Fiber, **19.5g** Sugars, **16.9g** Protein

CHEF'S NOTE: If your sweet potatoes or chickpeas come out a little too dry, serve with a dollop of plain vegan yogurt or hummus.

Chickpea Marinara 30 G S ⬭ $

Serves 2 | The garbanzo bean goes to Italy! Serve these Italian-flavored chickpeas over cooked pasta (or spaghetti squash for a low-carb option) or cooked greens, or on fresh whole-wheat Italian bread!

1 8-oz can tomato sauce
2 tsp Italian seasoning
1 tsp onion powder
    (granulated)
1 tsp garlic powder
    (granulated)
dash of black pepper
pinch of salt (optional)
hot sauce
1 15-oz can chickpeas,
    drained and rinsed
agave nectar or sugar, to
    taste (optional)

1. In a skillet (yes, a skillet!) whisk tomato sauce and seasonings, including a few drops of hot sauce.

2. Turn heat to medium-low and gently heat.

3. Once thoroughly warm, taste. If it's too acidic, add a drop of agave nectar or pinch of sugar (all tomato sauces are slightly different).

4. Add chickpeas, stirring to coat the chickpeas with the tomato sauce.

5. Reduce heat to low and continue to cook for a few minutes, stirring occasionally to incorporate the chickpeas with the sauce.

6. Once the chickpeas are warm and start to take on a little color from the tomato sauce, serve.

NUTRITIONAL INFORMATION 🥄 **304** Calories, **4g** Fat, **56.7g** Carbohydrates, **11.3g** Fiber, **6g** Sugars, **12.4g** Protein

Chickpea Tikka Masala ㉚ Ⓖ Ⓢ ⬭ Ⓢ

Serves 2 | Chicken tikka masala is a popular comfort food in Britain, known for its rich, creamy tomato sauce with hints of lemon and coriander. I've recreated the flavorful dish here, using chickpeas and silken tofu instead of yogurt.

6 oz silken tofu
1 tbsp fresh lemon juice
2 tsp ground cumin
1 tsp paprika
½ tsp onion powder (granulated)
½ tsp garlic powder (granulated)
¼ tsp ground cinnamon
¼ tsp ground ginger
½ tsp garam masala
⅛ tsp turmeric for color (optional)
1 8-oz can tomato sauce
cayenne powder or hot sauce, to taste
salt and pepper, to taste
1 15-oz can chickpeas, drained and rinsed
minced cilantro for garnish
cooked brown rice, as desired

1. Blend tofu with lemon juice, adding water as necessary until it reaches a creamy consistency.

2. In a medium saucepan, whisk spices, through turmeric, with tomato sauce.

3. Cover and heat over low until just warm, about 5 minutes.

4. Stir in blended tofu, whisking to combine.

5. Add cayenne powder or hot sauce (such as Tabasco, not Sriracha) to taste, plus salt and pepper to taste.

6. Add chickpeas and continue to heat over low until chickpeas are warm.

7. Garnish with cilantro and serve over rice. An additional dollop of yogurt on top is also delicious.

CHEF'S NOTE: For a soy-free version and one-pot meal, use plain coconut- or rice-based vegan yogurt (preferably unsweetened) instead of the silken tofu and lemon juice.

NUTRITIONAL INFORMATION (WITHOUT RICE) ⬱ **347** Calories, **3.4g** Fat, **64.3g** Carbohydrates, **12g** Fiber, **12.1g** Sugars, **17.7g** Protein

Skillet Frijoles Negros

Serves 2 | Black beans, those found in the Caribbean or Mexico, are soaked for 18 hours before cooking and then slow-cooked all day. Here I've shortened the process down to about 15 minutes, without sacrificing any of the flavor. For a complete meal, serve with a side of rice and a crisp salad or pico de gallo.

1 small sweet onion, diced
2 garlic cloves, minced
1 to 2 tsp minced fresh
   ginger
1 tsp chili powder
½ tsp ground cumin
dash of paprika
dash of ground cinnamon
1 15-oz can black beans,
   undrained
hot sauce or cayenne
   powder, to taste
fresh lime juice and zest,
   to taste (optional)
salt and pepper, to taste

CHEF'S NOTE:
A few dashes of
ground ginger may
be substituted for
the fresh ginger.

1. Line a skillet with a thin layer of water and sauté onion, garlic, and fresh ginger over high heat until onion is translucent and most of the water has cooked off, about 2 minutes.

2. Add chili powder, cumin, a light dash of paprika, and a very light dash of cinnamon, stirring to coat everything.

3. Continue to cook for about a minute, until fragrant and most of the liquid has cooked off. Add beans (with juices) and stir to combine.

4. Reduce heat to low and mash beans well with a fork or potato masher a few times. You still want some whole and half beans and not a refried consistency. It will look very soupy—don't be alarmed.

5. Crank the heat up to high and bring to a boil.

6. Once boiling, reduce heat to medium-high and cook for 10 minutes. If it's popping, cover for a few minutes, until it cooks down and stops popping. Stir the beans every minute or so, taking care to scrape the bottom and lift the beans. After 10 minutes the mixture should have significantly reduced. It may still be a little soupy, that is all right—it will thicken as it cools—but if it's really soupy, cook longer.

7. Add hot sauce (or cayenne powder) and lime juice and zest to taste. Season with salt and pepper and serve.

NUTRITIONAL INFORMATION 191 Calories, **0.5g** Fat, **30.4g** Carbohydrates, **6.2g** Fiber, **1.6g** Sugars, **9.1g** Protein

Pinquito Beans

Serves 2 | Also called Santa Maria Barbecue Beans, Pinquito Beans are basically baked beans with a Mexican twist. For a complete meal, serve with a side of rice such as Arroz Amarillo (pg. 162) and a salad or cooked greens.

1 small sweet onion, finely diced
3 garlic cloves, minced
1 14-oz can diced tomatoes, undrained
1 c Enchilada Sauce (pg. 284)
1 tbsp yellow mustard
½ tsp chili powder
light brown or raw sugar (optional)
1 15-oz can pinto beans, drained and rinsed

1. Line a medium pot with a thin layer of water and sauté onion and garlic over high heat until onion is translucent, about 2 minutes.

2. Add tomatoes (with juices), Enchilada Sauce, mustard, and chili powder, stirring to combine.

3. Bring to a boil for a minute, then taste, adding a little sugar if the tomato is too acidic or you prefer a sweeter baked bean.

4. Add beans, cover, and simmer for 10 minutes. Serve warm or cold.

CHEF'S NOTE: Pinquito Beans are traditionally made with pinquito beans (hence the name). Since pinquito beans are fairly hard to come by, I've substituted pinto beans, which I like better anyhow.

NUTRITIONAL INFORMATION 🥄 **293** Calories, **0.7g** Fat, **59.2g** Carbohydrates, **20.9g** Fiber, **16.4g** Sugars, **17.4g** Protein

Chickpea Tenders

Makes 4 | I think I lived off chicken tenders in college and I've wanted to replicate them for eons. I finally got around to doing it when I was writing this cookbook and now I'm sorry I waited so long!

1 15-oz can chickpeas,
   drained and rinsed
1 tsp Poultry Seasoning
   Mix (pg. 276)
2 tbsp + 1 tsp No-Chicken
   Broth Powder (pg. 299)
1 tsp Dijon mustard
1 tbsp Vegan Mayo
   (pg. 272)
1 tsp low-sodium soy sauce
⅓ cup vital wheat gluten
3 tbsp water

1. Preheat oven to 350°F.
2. Line a cookie sheet with parchment paper and set aside.
3. In a mixing bowl, mash beans with a fork until no whole beans are left. You want it mostly like refried beans.
4. Mix all ingredients together except gluten and water, until well combined.
5. Add gluten and water and mix.
6. Knead a few times with your hands and then let rest for a few minutes.
7. Divide dough into 4 equal parts using your hands and shape each into a thin, long, oval shape (like a chicken breast).
8. Bake for 10 minutes, flip, bake for 10 more minutes, and repeat both cycles, baking for a total of 40 minutes. Be careful not to burn: once they are firm and a nice golden brown, they are done.

CHEF'S NOTE:
A word of caution: do not substitute boullion for the No-Chicken Broth Powder as your tenders will come out too salty.

CHEF'S NOTE: I love eating leftovers cold on a sandwich with barbecue sauce or "Honey" Mustard (pg. 269).

NUTRITIONAL INFORMATION (1 TENDER) 186 Calories, 1.7g Fat, 28.9g Carbohydrates, 6g Fiber, 0g Sugars, 15g Protein

Cuban Black Bean Cakes

Makes 4 | These bean cakes capture traditional Cuban flavors and finish with a refreshing lime cream sauce. Since they're so easy and effortless to make, you'll be hooked on them in no time. The refreshing Lime Crème dressing is compliments of my dear friend Jane, who rules at all things lime-flavored.

1 15-oz can black beans, drained and rinsed
¼ c loosely packed fresh cilantro, chopped
1 tbsp ketchup
1 tsp garlic powder (granulated)
1 tsp onion powder (granulated)
½ tsp chili powder
½ tsp ground cumin
½ tsp dried oregano
2 tbsp Vegan Mayo (pg. 272)
2 tbsp cornmeal
Lime Crème (pg. 271)

1. Preheat oven to 350°F. Grease or line a cookie sheet with parchment paper and set aside.

2. In a mixing bowl, mash beans with a fork so that no whole beans are left but the mixture is not mushy and pureed like refried beans. Add cilantro, ketchup, spices, and Vegan Mayo and mix together.

3. Then add 1 tablespoon cornmeal and mix. If it's still slightly sticky to the touch, add another 1 teaspoon to 1 tablespoon of cornmeal. Try not to exceed 2 tablespoons of cornmeal, as it will dry the patties out.

4. Shape mixture into 4 patties (slightly smaller than a medium-size burger) using your hands.

5. Bake for 10 minutes, flip, and bake for 5 minutes more. Bake a third time for 5+ minutes. The patties should have a lightly crisp outside, but still be relatively soft, like crab cakes. You also don't want to overcook or your cakes will dry out.

6. Serve cakes with a dollop of Lime Crème.

NUTRITIONAL INFORMATION (1 CAKE) **111** Calories, **0.3g** Fat, **18.2g** Carbohydrates, **3.1g** Fiber, **1.9g** Sugars, **5.2g** Protein

"Crab" Cakes 30 G

Makes 5 | *Pictured opposite and on pg. 170* | One of the things I love most about tofu is how universal it can be. Add some oyster mushrooms and kelp for a fishy flavor, and voilà! Tofu that tastes like crab. This is my vegan version of Maryland's famous crab cake—except it's baked, not fried.

1 lb extra-firm tofu

3 celery stalks, shredded or minced

1¼ c oyster mushrooms, coarsely chopped

4 tbsp Vegan Mayo (pg. 272)

1 tsp onion powder (granulated)

½ tsp garlic powder (granulated)

¾ c instant oats

1 tsp kelp

1 tbsp low-sodium soy sauce

1 tbsp Old Bay seasoning

¼ tsp black pepper

juice of 1 to 2 lemon wedges

Rémoulade (pg. 271)

1. Press the tofu for 20 minutes, if possible. Shred tofu using a cheese grater or the shredding blade on a food processor. Transfer to a large mixing bowl.

3. Shred celery or mince by hand, and chop mushrooms.

4. Combine all ingredients through pepper together using your hands. Mix for at least a few minutes, particularly if you shredded the tofu with a cheese grater, so the strands break down. You want the mixture to be very crumbly, almost like cottage cheese.

5. Set aside and let rest while oven preheats to 350°F. Taste, adding more Old Bay or kelp if desired to get a fishier or spicier taste. Lightly grease a cookie sheet or line with parchment paper.

6. Pack some of the mixture firmly into a wide ½-cup measuring cup, then transfer molded cake to a cookie sheet. Repeat, until you have 5 cakes. If you don't have a wide measuring cup, just use your palm to lightly smoosh down the patty and shape into a round crab cake.

7. Squeeze the juice from a lemon wedge or two over the patties before baking. (You can also spray briefly with oil spray if you are worried about them drying out.)

8. Bake for 25 to 35 minutes, until outside is golden brown and crisp. Make Remoulade and lightly smear on each cake.

NUTRITIONAL INFORMATION (1 CAKE, WITHOUT SAUCE) 78 Calories, 1.3g Fat, 7.7g Carbohydrates, 1g Fiber, 2.1g Sugars, 8.8g Protein

Cajun Chickpea Cakes

Makes 8 | A contestant on *Top Chef* made Cajun chickpea cakes during an episode and I thought, "Oooh! That sounds delightful!" and set out to make my own. These cakes, which were featured on Happyherbivore.com back in 2009, remain one of my favorite go-to meals, since they're made with cheap pantry staples and are complemented by just about any side of veggies.

1 15-oz can chickpeas,
   drained and rinsed
2 tbsp Vegan Mayo
   (pg. 272)
1 tbsp Poultry Seasoning
   Mix (pg. 276)
1 tbsp chili powder
1 tbsp tamari
1 tbsp fresh lime juice
¼ tsp garlic powder
   (granulated)
¼ tsp onion powder
   (granulated)
¼ tsp paprika
¼ tsp liquid smoke
⅛ tsp cayenne powder
¼ c chickpea flour
Smoky Cajun Mayo
   (optional; pg. 267)

1. Preheat oven to 350°F.
2. Line a cookie sheet with parchment paper and set aside.
3. Place chickpeas in a food processor and pulse about 10 times, until they are coarsely chopped but not pureed (you can also try this with a fork).
4. Transfer chickpeas and all remaining ingredients to a mixing bowl and stir to combine.
5. Roll 8 balls, then spray lightly with cooking spray.
6. Place balls 4 inches apart on the cookie sheet and flatten gently with the palm of your hand.
7. Lightly respray the cakes and sprinkle with additional salt if desired.
8. Bake for 12 to 15 minutes, until thoroughly warm and a bit crispy.
9. Serve with Smoky Cajun Mayo or another condiment or sauce.

CHEF'S NOTE: Low-sodium soy sauce may be substituted for the tamari and white whole-wheat flour may be substituted for the chickpea flour, though the chickpea flour is preferable.

NUTRITIONAL INFORMATION (1 CAKE) **95** Calories, **1.2g** Fat, **17.4g** Carbohydrates, **3.9g** Fiber, **1.2g** Sugars, **4.4g** Protein

Cajun Black-Eyed Pea Cakes

Makes 5 | A black-eyed pea got into a tussle with a crab cake during Mardi Gras. Or something like that.

2 tbsp Creamy Cajun
   Mustard (pg. 269)
1 15-oz can black-eyed
   peas, drained and rinsed
1 celery stalk, minced
2 tbsp ketchup
1 tsp onion powder
   (granulated)
1 tsp Cajun Seasoning
   (pg. 277)
¼ tsp black pepper
2 tbsp instant oats

1. Prepare Creamy Cajun Mustard and set aside.

2. Preheat oven to 350°F.

3. Lightly grease a cookie sheet or line with parchment paper and set aside.

4. Mash beans with a fork so no whole beans are left, but still some half beans. You don't want it too chunky, but you also don't want the consistency of refried beans.

5. Mix beans with all remaining ingredients, except oats, until well combined, then add oats.

6. Shape into 5 small patties (slightly smaller than a veggie burger) and place on cookie sheet.

7. Bake for 10 minutes, flip, and bake for 7 minutes more. Repeat a third time if necessary, checking after 5 minutes. The cakes should have a slightly crisp outer shell, but should still be soft in the middle (think crab cakes).

8. Serve with a little spread (smear) of Creamy Cajun Mustard on each cake.

> CHEF'S NOTE: Rolled oats may be substituted for instant oats if you chop them up in your food processor first.

NUTRITIONAL INFORMATION (1 CAKE) 🍠 **99** Calories, **1.4g** Fat, **14.2g** Carbohydrates, **2.8g** Fiber, **0.9g** Sugars, **4.7g** Protein

Indian Spiced Chickpeas & Kale

Serves 2 | I'm one of those vegans that could eat kale three times a day—I freely admit that. I don't know when it happened, I didn't always eat kale so obsessively, but I can't ever seem to get enough of it. Indian food also happens to be one of my favorite cuisines to cook—and eat—so it makes sense that I blended these two faves in a quick weeknight meal.

2 c kale, chopped
2 garlic cloves, minced
¼ c tomato sauce
1 tbsp water or broth
½ tsp ground cumin
¼ tsp ground coriander
⅛ tsp ground ginger
pinch of salt
1 c cooked chickpeas
⅛ to ¼ teaspoon garam
   masala (optional)
few dashes of garlic
   powder (granulated)
   (optional)

1. Steam kale until it's bright green and slightly softer, about 3 to 5 minutes. Set kale aside on a plate.

2. Combine garlic through salt in a skillet and cook over medium heat for 5 minutes.

3. Add chickpeas and stir to coat, adding another tablespoon water if necessary.

4. Cook until warm.

5. Remove from heat and stir in garam masala and set aside for a few minutes.

6. Plate kale and sprinkle generously with garlic powder (optional). Top with chickpeas and serve.

> **CHEF'S NOTE:** I prefer to use an electric steamer to steam my kale, but you can line a large pot with a thin layer of water, bringing it to a boil, add kale and cover until it's bright green, stirring once or twice to promote even cooking.

NUTRITIONAL INFORMATION 🥄 **166** Calories, **1.8g** Fat, **32.1g** Carbohydrates, **6.3g** Fiber, **1.3g** Sugars, **7.8g** Protein

Veggie Lo Mein

Serves 2 | Better than greasy takeout, this lo mein is healthy and uses up whatever stir-fry veggies you have on hand. You can also use any kind of noodle you like here, such as soba, udon, spaghetti, or linguine.

LO MEIN SAUCE:
2 tbsp low-sodium soy
  sauce
1 tsp rice vinegar
dash of ground ginger
dash of garlic powder
  (granulated)
drop of agave nectar
¼ tsp Asian hot sauce

LO MEIN:
3 oz Asian noodles
5 green onions
2 garlic cloves, minced
1 tbsp minced fresh ginger
pinch of red pepper flakes
1 c sliced mushrooms
  (optional)
Other vegetables of your
  choice (optional)
1 to 2 c stir-fry veggies

1. Prepare noodles according to package instructions.

2. Meanwhile, whisk all ingredients for Lo Mein Sauce together and set aside.

3. Cut the roots and dark green stalks off the onions. Discard the roots and save the stalks for another use. Cut the white and light green parts into 2-inch pieces and then slice in half lengthwise; set aside.

4. Line a large skillet with a thin layer of water. Bring to a boil and add onions, garlic, ginger, and red pepper flakes.

5. After a minute, add mushrooms and other vegetables and continue to cook until everything is al dente: cooked but still crisp. Add a little water as necessary to prevent sticking but use the least amount possible.

6. Once everything is cooked, toss with prepared noodles and pour Lo Mein Sauce over top, stirring to coat and evenly distribute everything.

NUTRITIONAL INFORMATION (WITH NOODLES) **200** Calories, **0.8g** Fat, **43g** Carbohydrates, **2.8g** Fiber, **3.3g** Sugars, **9.6g** Protein

Creamy Dijon Pasta

Serves 2 | Using tofu to make a cream sauce for pasta not only cuts the fat, it adds protein to an otherwise carb-heavy dish. Frozen peas make this dish evergreen, but you can substitute asparagus and tomatoes when they're in season.

4 oz whole-wheat
   spaghetti
2 c frozen peas
6 oz silken tofu
2 tbsp Dijon mustard
1 tbsp apple cider vinegar
dash of ground nutmeg
   (optional)
black pepper, to taste

1. Cook pasta according to package instructions, tossing peas or asparagus into the cooking water a few minutes before the pasta is done to warm and/or cook the veggies.

2. Meanwhile, combine tofu, mustard, vinegar, and optional nutmeg in a blender.

3. Whiz until smooth and creamy, adding 1 to 2 tablespoons of water if necessary.

4. Toss warm pasta and veggies with the cream sauce and garnish with freshly ground black pepper before serving.

> **CHEF'S NOTE:** Any pasta shape and gluten-free pasta may be substituted here. Half a package of Mori-Nu tofu (any firmness) may also be substituted for the silken tofu.

NUTRITIONAL INFORMATION 🥄 **261** Calories, **3.7g** Fat, **40.9g** Carbohydrates, **12g** Fiber, **9.2g** Sugars, **17.8g** Protein

Quick Pumpkin-Sage Pasta

Serves 2 | This is a great way to use up leftover pumpkin. It whips up as quickly as you can boil pasta and really captures the taste of autumn. By the way, you can use the rest of your pumpkin and fresh sage to make Harvest Cornbread (pg. 65).

4 oz whole-wheat pasta
¾ c vegetable broth
¾ c canned pure pumpkin
1 to 2 tbsp minced fresh
   sage
½ tsp pumpkin pie spice
pinch of dried oregano
pinch of red pepper
   flakes (optional)
salt and pepper, to taste
vegan Parmesan for
   garnish (optional)

1. Cook pasta according to package instructions.

2. Meanwhile, combine remaining ingredients together in a small saucepan and heat over low until thoroughly warm, about 5 minutes.

3. Taste, adding more sage if desired plus salt and pepper to taste.

4. Cover and let sauce rest for 5 to 10 minutes, allowing the flavors to merge and sauce to thicken slightly.

5. Toss cooked pasta with pumpkin sauce and taste, adding more salt and pepper as needed. Garnish with vegan Parmesan if desired.

> **CHEF'S NOTE:** For a one-pot meal, prepare sauce in the same pot used to cook pasta, setting the pasta aside as you make the sauce.

NUTRITIONAL INFORMATION (WITH 2 OZ PASTA) 🍜 **262** Calories, **2.4g** Fat, **51g** Carbohydrates, **8.2g** Fiber, **5.3g** Sugars, **10g** Protein

Lemon Basil Pasta 30 F G S ⬓ $

Serves 2 | *Pictured opposite and on pg. 192* | I created this dish back in college and served it any time I wanted to impress someone (read: cute boys). I like to serve this in the summer because it's light and refreshing. To round out the dish and add a bit of color, add fresh baby spinach or asparagus spears before serving.

8 oz whole-wheat spaghetti
1 pint cherry tomatoes,
    sliced in half
juice of 1 lemon
¼ c fresh basil, chopped
2 tbsp capers
black pepper, to taste
1 basil leaf for garnish
    (optional)

CHEF'S NOTE:
For a gluten-free dish,
use gluten-free pasta

1. Cook pasta according to the package instructions. A minute before the pasta is done, add the tomatoes to the cooking water to cook with the pasta. You want the tomatoes to soften slightly but still be fairly crisp.

2. Drain, and rinse pasta and tomatoes briefly with cool water so the pasta is still warm, but not boiling hot.

3. Return the pasta to the pot and add the lemon juice, fresh basil, and 2 tablespoons of capers; mix to combine. You can add another tablespoon of capers if you really like the taste and contrast.

4. Garnish with fresh black pepper and a nice basil leaf.

CHEF'S NOTE: For a stronger lemon flavor, add lemon zest to the pasta.

CHEF'S NOTE: This pasta dish is also great chilled and the flavor intensifies the next day, so look forward to leftovers.

NUTRITIONAL INFORMATION 🐟 **174** Calories, **1g** Fat, **37.8g** Carbohydrates, **7.3g** Fiber, **5.2g** Sugars, **7.7g** Protein

Quick Pesto

Makes 1½ cups | This pesto sauce comes together in an instant and is great for tiresome weeknights when the only thing you're capable of doing is boiling pasta. To round out the meal, add any of the following: canned artichoke hearts, quartered; hearts of palm, sliced; cherry tomatoes, sliced; kalamata olives, sliced; broccoli florets; or asparagus spears, sliced.

6 oz plain vegan yogurt
1 c fresh basil leaves,
   packed tight
1 garlic clove
juice of 1 lemon wedge
salt and pepper, to taste

1 Combine yogurt, basil, and garlic in a blender or food processor and puree until smooth, creamy, and a brilliant green.

2 Taste. If the yogurt was sweetened and the pesto is a little sweet for your taste, add lemon (about ¼ teaspoon of juice). You can also add more basil here if the pesto is not as strong as you'd like. Add salt and pepper. Toss ¼ cup of pesto with cooked pasta (slightly warm or lightly chilled but not piping hot), adding more pesto as necessary until the pasta is well coated, or use the pesto as a sandwich spread, as a pizza sauce, a dip, or any way you enjoy pesto.

CHEF'S NOTE:
If you can't find commercial vegan yogurt, try using 1 cup of soft or silken tofu.

CHEF'S NOTE:
The more basil, the merrier—you really want to pack your measuring cup full of basil.

VARIATION

Spinach Pesto 30 F G S $ 🥄 Substitute 2 cups of fresh spinach (baby spinach, or chopped with stems removed) for the basil, but you'll want to add more garlic cloves (to taste) to balance out the spinach flavor.

NUTRITIONAL INFORMATION

QUICK PESTO (¼ C) 🥄 **20** Calories, **0.5g** Fat, **2.3g** Carbohydrates, **0g** Fiber, **2g** Sugars, **1.7g** Protein

SPINACH PESTO (¼ C) 🥄 **16** calories **0.4g** Fat, **1.9g** Carbohydrates, **0g** Fiber, **1.5g** Sugars, **1.4g** Protein

Chili–Sweet Mango Noodles

Serves 2 | Fruit stands are all over Los Angeles the way hot dog carts are all over Manhattan. Sometimes the vendors will sprinkle hot spices over the fruit, and it's that sweet-to-spicy contrast I've incorporated here, in an Asian-inspired dish.

6 oz udon noodles
1 bunch green onions
1 c vegetable broth, divided
2 garlic cloves, minced
¼ tsp red pepper flakes
2 tbsp low-sodium soy sauce
2 tbsp rice vinegar
1 tbsp sweet red chili sauce
3 tsp fresh minced ginger
1 mango, skinned and cubed

CHEF'S NOTE:
Udon noodles are thick, flat, wheat-based Japanese noodles. Thick brown-rice noodles may be substituted for convenience or a gluten-free option.

1. Prepare noodles according to package directions, rinsing with cold water, draining, and setting aside.

2. Cut the dark green stalk and root end off the green onions, tossing the roots, but reserving the stalks for later. Slice the remaining white and light green parts of the onions in half and then in half again, so each piece is about 2 inches long, and set aside.

3. Pour ⅓ cup of vegetable broth into a large skillet and add garlic, a pinch of red pepper flakes, low-sodium soy sauce, and vinegar; stir to combine. Taste, adding more low-sodium soy sauce if desired.

4. Bring to a boil over high heat and sauté for 2 minutes. Add chopped green onions and cook for another minute. Add another ⅓ cup of broth, red chili sauce, and ginger and cook for another minute or two, stirring to combine everything.

5. Turn off heat and add remaining broth if necessary. You want a slight sauce in the pan—a thin layer along the bottom. Taste, adding more red chili sauce is desired.

6. Add mango and cooked noodles, stirring to combine.

7. Move the mixture away from heat and let flavors merge in the skillet. Slice leftover green onion parts on the diagonal. Reserve a few onion slices, but stir the rest into the noodle dish. Plate, garnish, and serve.

NUTRITIONAL INFORMATION 🍜 **412** Calories, **2.9g** Fat, **82.9g** Carbohydrates, **8.1g** Fiber, **24.6g** Sugars, **15.5g** Protein

Sun-Dried Tomato Cream Sauce

Makes 1 cup | This rich and creamy sauce is perfect over pasta on a busy week night. If you can, make it ahead—the flavors intensify the next day.

¼ c sun-dried tomatoes
1 c nondairy milk
¼ c nutritional yeast
1 tsp yellow miso
½ tsp onion powder
    (granulated)
dash of paprika
¼ tsp Cajun Seasoning
    (pg. 277)
pinch of salt
few dashes of black pepper
1 garlic clove
juice of 1 lemon slice
basil flakes or chopped
    fresh basil for garnish
    (optional)

1. Rehydrate tomatoes by filling a small saucepan with water halfway and bringing it to a boil.

2. Once boiling, add tomatoes and turn off heat. Tomatoes should be ready in about 10 minutes.

3. Drain water off and combine rehydrated tomatoes with remaining ingredients in a blender and puree until smooth.

4. Transfer to a saucepan and gently warm over low heat.

5. Taste, whisking in another 1 to 2 tablespoons of nutritional yeast if desired.

6. Serve over pasta or use as a dunking sauce with crusty bread. Garnish with a few dried basil flakes or a pinch of chopped fresh basil if desired.

CHEF'S NOTE: If you use unsweetened nondairy milk, you may need add a drop or two of agave nectar or a pinch of sugar to take the acidic edge off the sun-dried tomatoes.

CHEF'S NOTE: Tomato sauce can be used in place of the sun-dried tomatoes if you're in a pinch, but sun-dried tomatoes are preferable.

NUTRITIONAL INFORMATION (¼ C) 76 Calories, **1.7g** Fat, **10.2g** Carbohydrates, **3.1g** Fiber, **3.3g** Sugars, **7.3g** Protein

Pablo Pasta 30 Ⓖ 🍲 $

Serves 3 | This is a slightly spicy south-of-the-border take on mac 'n' cheese. You can make it as spicy as you like by adding more green chilies, red pepper flakes, or hot sauce. Don't let the long ingredients list scare you off. It's mostly spices.

1¼ c whole-wheat pasta
1¼ c nondairy milk
⅓ c nutritional yeast
2 tbsp yellow miso
2 tbsp cornstarch
1 tsp onion powder
    (granulated)
1 tsp garlic powder
    (granulated)
½ tsp paprika
½ tsp ground cumin
¼ tsp turmeric
pinch of red pepper flakes
2 tbsp minced green chilies
2 tbsp tomato sauce
1 15-oz can black beans,
    drained and rinsed
chopped tomatoes for
    garnish (optional)
1 sliced green onion for
    garnish (optional)
hot sauce, to taste
    (optional)

1. Cook pasta according to package instructions, immediately drain, rinse with cold water, and set aside.

2. Whisk nondairy milk, nutritional yeast, miso, cornstarch, spices, green chilies (adding more if you like), and tomato sauce together in a saucepan.

3. Heat over medium heat and bring to a near-boil, then turn heat down to low and allow to thicken, stirring occasionally.

4. Taste, adding more red pepper flakes (or hot sauce) as desired.

5. Stir in beans and pasta, until everything is well coated.

6. Garnish with tomatoes, green onion slices, and a splash of hot sauce.

> **CHEF'S NOTE:** Gluten-free pasta or any pasta shape can be used here but tubular pasta, such as elbow macaroni or ziti, works best.

> **CHEF'S NOTE:** To make this a one-pot meal, prepare sauce in the same pot you used to cook pasta.

NUTRITIONAL INFORMATION 🍽 **401** Calories, **2.9g** Fat, **68g** Carbohydrates, **12.4g** Fiber, **8.3g** Sugars, **23.1g** Protein

Pasta with Braised Vegetables 30 G S

Serves 2 | I was raised on pasta, and while I love marinara sauce, sometimes I want a change of pace. That's where this dish comes in. Balsamic vinegar, asparagus, tomatoes, and pasta? They belong together.

1 bunch asparagus
1 pint cherry tomatoes, sliced in half
3 garlic cloves, sliced thinly
4 oz whole-wheat pasta
3 dashes of garlic powder (granulated)
pinch of Italian seasoning
balsamic vinegar, to taste

CHEF'S NOTE: Gluten-free pastas can be used here, as can any pasta shape, but long noodles such as spaghetti and linguine work best.

1. Preheat oven to 425°F.

2. Trim the woody bottom (about the lower ⅓) off of the asparagus.

3. Line up asparagus on a cookie sheet, spritz lightly with oil spray and sprinkle generously with salt and pepper. Shake the tray so the asparagus rotate, then spray and season again. Add tomatoes and garlic, scattering them about, but take care to place garlic on top of the asparagus.

4. Bake for 10 to 15 minutes, until asparagus is cooked and tender, but still crisp and bright green. Garlic should be golden around the edges and the tomatoes should be soft.

5. Meanwhile, cook pasta according to package directions and drain.

6. While pasta is still hot, toss with a few dashes of garlic powder and a good pinch of Italian seasoning.

7. Drizzle a little balsamic over cooked veggies and toss to coat, adding more balsamic until there is a light coating on the pasta and veggies, or to taste.

NUTRITIONAL INFORMATION 262 Calories, **1.9g** Fat, **52.7g** Carbohydrates, **8.4g** Fiber, **7.4g** Sugars, **10.3g** Protein

Tofu Ricotta

Makes 2 cups | I love this ricotta for my salads, but it also really jazzes up a plain bowl of pasta with marinara while adding a good bit of protein to a usually carb-heavy dish.

1 lb extra-firm tofu
¼ c nutritional yeast
½ tsp yellow or white miso (optional)
1 tsp lemon juice
1 tbsp Italian seasoning
¼ tsp onion powder (granulated)
¼ tsp garlic powder (granulated)
black pepper, to taste

1. Give tofu a good squeeze, pressing out any excess moisture, then crumble into a mixing bowl using your hands.

2. Add remaining ingredients and stir with a fork or your hands until well combined.

3. Taste, adding another 1 tablespoon of nutritional yeast if desired, plus more miso, lemon juice, or Italian seasoning to taste.

4. Add fresh black pepper and serve.

NUTRITIONAL INFORMATION (¼ C) ☜ **25** Calories, **0.8g** Fat, **2.8g** Carbohydrates, **1.3g** Fiber, **0g** Sugars, **2.5g** Protein

Simple Sides

Cauliflower Manchurian 30

Serves 2 | This cauliflower dish blends Asian and Indian flavors beautifully. It has a rich and complex flavor, but is slightly sweet and also a little spicy. I like to serve this as a side dish, but you can turn it into a full meal by doubling the sauce and tossing it with chickpeas and 2 cups of peas. Then serve it over brown rice.

1 head cauliflower, cut into florets
3 tbsp ketchup
2 tbsp sweet red chili sauce
1 tsp garam masala
2 tsp garlic powder (granulated)
¼ + ⅛ tsp ground ginger
2 tsp low-sodium soy sauce

1. Line a large pot with a thin layer of water and bring to a boil.
2. Once boiling, add cauliflower and turn heat to medium-low.
3. Continue to cook, adding more water if necessary, until cauliflower is soft and fork-tender, but not falling apart.
4. Meanwhile, combine remaining ingredients in a small bowl.
5. Taste, adding more chili sauce or garam masala as desired (both vary slightly by brand).
6. Once the cauliflower is cooked, drain off excess water and dump sauce over the top.
7. Stir several times using a spatula or large spoon to make sure all the cauliflower is evenly coated, and serve.

CHEF'S NOTE: For a rustic texture and nutty flavor, roast cauliflower for 35 to 40 minutes at 420°F instead of steaming.

NUTRITIONAL INFORMATION 69 Calories, 0.3g Fat, 15.5g Carbohydrates, 3.8g Fiber, 9.3g Sugars, 4g Protein

Gingered Collard Greens

Serves 2 | This is one of my favorite Ethiopian dishes. Although I normally like to drown my collard greens in hot sauce, a local Ethiopian restaurant showed me how fresh ginger really complements the greens' unique taste. You can also substitute any greens you like here, but I like collard greens the best.

pinch of red pepper flakes
2 garlic cloves, minced
⅓ c finely chopped red
    onion
2 tbsp minced fresh ginger
2 c chopped collard greens
salt and pepper, to taste
hot sauce (optional)

1. Line a large pot with a thin layer of water—the thinnest layer possible. Bring to a boil and sauté a good pinch of red pepper flakes for 30 seconds.

2. Add garlic and onion and cook for another minute.

3. Add ginger and then collards, using tongs or a spatula to flip and move the greens around. Add splashes of water as necessary and continue to cook until the collards are bright green, or cook them longer if you prefer a well-cooked and soft green.

4. Season generously with salt and pepper.

5. Give it a good stir and serve with hot sauce on the table.

NUTRITIONAL INFORMATION   **42** Calories, **0.5g** Fat, **8.7g** Carbohydrates, **2.4g** Fiber, **1.2g** Sugars, **1.8g** Protein

Roasted Carrots $

Serves 4 | My go-to side dish. Sure, steamed carrots are easy, but roasted carrots are so much tastier! I love to use baby carrots in this dish.

16 oz baby carrots
salt and pepper, to taste
onion powder
　(granulated), to taste

> **CHEF'S NOTE:**
> You can add a pinch or two of dried herbs or Italian seasoning for a more complex dish.

> **CHEF'S NOTE:**
> If using regular-sized carrots, cut them down into smaller pieces before starting, about the size of baby carrots.

1. Preheat oven to 400°F.
2. If your baby carrots are rather big, cut in half lengthwise.
3. Fill your baking dish (any size) with baby carrots so there is no overlap.
4. Spritz lightly with oil spray and shake the tray so the carrots rotate. Spritz again. Repeat a third time if necessary (but try not to).
5. Sprinkle generously with salt, pepper, and onion powder. Shake and sprinkle again. Repeat a third time, or until all carrots are well coated in the seasonings. Make sure there is no overlap, using your fingers to move carrots as necessary.
6. Bake for 20 to 35 minutes, until carrots are fork-tender.
7. Spritz with oil spray halfway through baking to prevent them from drying out.

> **CHEF'S NOTE:** These carrots were especially popular with my testers' children and grandchildren.

NUTRITIONAL INFORMATION (1 C) 🥕 **32** Calories, **0.7g** Fat, **6.3g** Carbohydrates, **1.7g** Fiber, **3.1g** Sugars, **0.6g** Protein

Garlicky Spinach 30 G S $ 1

Serves 1 | Mmmm, garlic. Plain old spinach starts to bore me after a while, but pile it high with garlic and I can't get enough!

¼ c vegetable broth
6 cloves garlic, thinly sliced
1 tsp Dijon mustard
1 tsp red wine vinegar
pinch of red pepper flakes
10 oz baby spinach
salt and pepper, to taste

1. Line a skillet or large pot with the thinnest layer of broth possible.
2. Sauté garlic for a minute, then stir in mustard and vinegar.
3. Add red pepper flakes and continue to cook until the garlic takes on a more golden color.
4. Add spinach and a tiny bit more broth if necessary—just enough to keep it from sticking.
5. Continue to cook, stirring to help the spinach or other greens cook down.
6. Stir to incorporate everything and sprinkle with salt and pepper before serving.

CHEF'S NOTE: Any greens you like may be substituted for the spinach and feel free to add more garlic.

NUTRITIONAL INFORMATION **97** Calories, **1.4g** Fat, **16.7g** Carbohydrates, **6.9g** Fiber, **1.4g** Sugars, **9.5g** Protein

Sweet Slaw 30 F G 1

Serves 4 | Pictured on pg. 214 | I love this slaw because it comes together as fast as you can chop and it's really quite stunning. It's a fabulous side dish for four, but also makes a great lunchtime meal for one.

½ small red cabbage
1 golden apple
1 carrot, skinned
1 tbsp Vegan Mayo
    (pg. 272)
¼ c raisins (optional)

1. Shred or thinly slice cabbage and slice apple and carrot into matchsticks.

2. Mix together with 1 tablespoon of Vegan Mayo, making sure everything is evenly coated.

3. Add another ½ to 1 tablespoon of Vegan Mayo if necessary.

4. Sprinkle raisins on top and serve.

> **CHEF'S NOTE:** A little lemon, lime, or orange juice can add a nice citrusy dimension to this slaw.

NUTRITIONAL INFORMATION 🥄 **64** Calories, **0.2g** Fat; **16.5g** Carbohydrates, **2.7g** Fiber, **11.8g** Sugars, **1.1g** Protein

Maryland's Kale 30 F G S $

Serves 2 | Old Bay seasoning is my favorite topping for kale and here I've jazzed the dish up a little by adding sweet onions and a bit of fresh garlic.

1 bunch kale
1 small sweet onion, sliced
3 garlic cloves, minced
Old Bay seasoning
1 lemon wedge (optional)

1. Pull leaves away from kale stems and discard stems. Tear any large leaves into bite-size pieces. Rinse under cold water and set aside.

2. Line a large skillet with a thin layer of water and bring to a boil.

3. Once the water is boiling, add onion. After a minute, add garlic. Continue to cook for another minute.

4. Reduce heat to medium and add kale.

5. Cover and let kale steam.

6. Once most of the kale has turned a bright green, about 30 to 45 seconds, remove the lid and give it a good stir, so all kale pieces are bright green.

7. Remove from heat and sprinkle generously with Old Bay seasoning. Mix with tongs or a spoon and fork to incorporate the garlic and onion with the kale. Add more Old Bay seasoning to taste (I am very generous!) and serve with a lemon wedge, if desired.

> CHEF'S NOTE: Old Bay seasoning comes to us from Maryland, where it's primarily served with locally caught crabs. A lemon wedge is always served as a garnish in this signature dish, as fresh lemon juice adds a nice dimension to the flavors in the Old Bay seasoning—try it!

NUTRITIONAL INFORMATION 88 Calories, 1g Fat, 18.2g Carbohydrates, 3.4g Fiber, 1.5g Sugars, 5.1g Protein

Dijon Asparagus

Serves 4 | When I'm serving asparagus, I try to only add taste elements that enhance the natural flavor, such as balsamic vinegar or this tangy Dijon dressing.

1 bunch asparagus
1½ tbsp Dijon Mustard
2 tbsp vegetable broth
salt and pepper, to taste

CHEF'S NOTE:
See pg. 210 (Braised
Veggies/Pasta page)
for baking asparagus
instructions.

1. Trim the asparagus by removing the hard and woody bottom ⅓.

2. Bake or steam the asparagus until it turns bright green and is just fork-tender, about 10 minutes. Be careful not to overcook, as asparagus quickly gets soggy and you want it slightly crisp.

3. Meanwhile, whisk Dijon with 1 tablespoon of broth at a time. You want it to be the consistency of a dressing: not as thick as mustard, but not as runny as broth. Toss dressing with asparagus to coat. Add salt and pepper to taste, then serve.

Cheater Asian Slaw

Serves 4 | *Pictured opposite* | This is another "cheater" recipe since it uses a dab of peanut butter, but it's a great side to any sandwich. You can also add mandarin oranges and shelled edamame to this slaw.

2 tbsp vegetable broth
2 tsp rice vinegar
1 tbsp smooth peanut
    butter
½ head small cabbage,
    very thinly sliced
1 carrot, skinned and
    julienned
lime wedges for garnish

1. Whisk broth, vinegar, and peanut butter together until smooth and creamy. Toss sauce with cabbage and carrot pieces until well combined.

2. Add any optional ingredients, toss quickly, and serve, garnished with crushed peanuts (if desired) and lime wedges.

CHEF'S NOTE: The sauce also makes a great
salad dressing.

NUTRITIONAL INFORMATION

DIJON ASPARAGUS 🥄 29 Calories, 0.4g Fat, 5g Carbohydrates, 2.7g Fiber, 2.3g Sugars, 3.1g Protein

CHEATER ASIAN SLAW 🥄 51 Calories, 2.1g Fat, 6.6g Carbohydrates, 2.5g Fiber, 3.5g Sugars, 2.1g Protein

Spicy Orange Greens

Serves 2 | The slightly spicy orange sauce in this dish is one of my favorites. You can serve it with any greens you like or have on hand, but collard greens are my favorite to use here. Broccoli florets may also be substituted. For a complete meal, serve over or tossed with soba noodles.

3 oz soba noodles
(optional)
⅓ c water
2 tbsp low-sodium soy
sauce
2 tbsp minced fresh
ginger
¼ tsp red pepper flakes
1 tbsp orange marmalade
4 c greens, chopped

1. Prepare noodles (if using) according to package instructions and set aside.

2. Pour water, low-sodium soy sauce, ginger, and red pepper flakes into a skillet. Turn heat to high and sauté ginger until fragrant, about a minute.

3. Whisk in marmalade and then add greens.

4. Reduce heat to medium and using tongs, flip the greens in the saucepan until they are bright green and have softened.

5. Toss the greens together with noodles, if using. Alternatively, toss sauce with cooked broccoli and noodles and serve.

CHEF'S NOTE: Soba noodles are Japanese noodles made from buckwheat flour. They are thin, somewhat like linguine, which can be substituted.

NUTRITIONAL INFORMATION (WITHOUT NOODLES) 156 Calories, 1.5g Fat, 32g Carbohydrates, 8.8g Fiber, 11.6g Sugars, 10.1g Protein

Caribbean Sweet Potatoes

Serves 4 | I found a great recipe for sweet potato wedges in our local St. Maarten newspaper (sxmfaxinfo.com). The recipe originally called for honey, which I replaced with an apple, and for various fresh herbs that I simplified with Italian seasoning.

½ tsp ground cinnamon
½ tsp ground ginger
¼ tsp chili powder, or more
dash or two of nutmeg
good pinch of Italian
    seasoning
2 small sweet potatoes,
    skinned and diced
1 red apple, cored and
    diced (skins optional)
juice of lime wedges
    (optional)
salt and pepper, to taste
    (optional)

1. Preheat oven to 400°F.
2. Line a cookie sheet with parchment paper, and set aside.
3. Whisk spices and Italian seasoning together in a small bowl and set aside.
4. Rinse potatoes and apples under cold water, then transfer to a large bowl and mix with spices.
5. If the pieces are not well coated, make a second batch of spices and mix.
6. Transfer to cookie sheet, avoiding any overlap.
7. Bake for 10 to 20 minutes, or until fork-tender and crisp.
8. Squeeze lime juice over the top, if desired.
9. Season lightly with salt and pepper if desired and serve.

CHEF'S NOTE: For a spicy kick, increase the chili powder to taste and add a little cayenne powder or hot sauce instead of lime juice at the end.

NUTRITIONAL INFORMATION 🥄 **161** Calories, **0.4g** Fat, **37.9g** Carbohydrates, **6.3g** Fiber, **14.5g** Sugars, **3.2g** Protein

Harvest Home Fries ③⓪ Ⓕ Ⓖ Ⓢ $

Serves 2 | In my last cookbook, I made these home fries savory with dried rosemary. Recently, I tried them with cinnamon and ohmigosh! It's like a dessert, but super healthy and perfect for brunch! To round out this meal, serve with Tempeh Sausage Crumbles (pg. 35).

2 medium sweet potatoes, cubed
1 small red apple, cored and diced
½ tsp ground cinnamon
salt and pepper, to taste

1 Preheat oven to 400°F.

2 Grease cookie sheet or line with parchment paper and set aside.

3 Rinse potatoes and apple pieces under cold water, then transfer to a mixing bowl.

4 Sprinkle cinnamon over top and then mix with your hands. Repeat, adding more cinnamon and mixing, until potatoes and apples are lightly coated.

5 Transfer to cookie sheet, making sure there is no overlap.

6 Spray quickly with cooking spray, if desired, and bake for 15 to 25 minutes, or until fully cooked and crisp.

7 Add salt and pepper immediately after baking.

> **CHEF'S NOTE:** I like to leave the skins on both the apples and potatoes for added nutrients and texture, but feel free to remove them.

NUTRITIONAL INFORMATION 🥄 **152** Calories, **0.3g** Fat, **36.9g** Carbohydrates, **6.4g** Fiber, **16.9g** Sugars, **2.6g** Protein

Cheesy Cauliflower Hash ㉚ Ⓕ Ⓖ Ⓢ Ⓢ

Serves 4 | One morning I tried to make "hash browns" out of cauliflower and ended up with this instead. It reminds me a lot of cheese grits and I feel good about eating a vegetable at breakfast. Don't limit this dish to breakfast, however; it also makes a terrific side dish to most meals.

1 head cauliflower, cut
   into florets
1 small sweet onion, diced
2 garlic cloves, minced
⅓ cup nutritional yeast
Cajun Seasoning
   (pg. 277)
hot sauce (optional)

1. Pulse cauliflower in a blender or food processor, in batches if necessary, until finely ground into thick crumbs, and set aside.

2. Line a large pot with a thin layer of water and sauté onion and garlic over high heat until translucent.

3. Add cauliflower and continue to cook, stirring frequently until it starts to soften.

4. Add nutritional yeast plus Cajun Seasoning and turn heat off.

5. Cover for a minute, then stir to incorporate.

6. Taste, adding more Cajun Seasoning, if desired, plus salt and pepper to taste.

7. Serve with hot sauce on the table.

> CHEF'S NOTE: I love to add extra veggies to this dish, particularly diced red bell peppers.

NUTRITIONAL INFORMATION ⬤ **140** Calories, **1.6g** Fat, **22.7g** Carbohydrates, **10.3g** Fiber, **4.7g** Sugars, **14.7g** Protein

Rainbow Greens

Serves 2 | I've always been attracted to rainbow chard (it's just so pretty!) but taste-wise it was my least favorite green, until I thought to pair it with raisins. The raisins add a nice sweetness to the dish, which helps mellow the earthy and sometimes bitter flavor chard can have. If you don't have access to chard, no problem! Any sturdy greens, like collards or kale, are a fine substitution. To turn this dish into a full meal, toss in chickpeas and serve with a grain such as quinoa or couscous.

1 bunch rainbow chard
4 garlic cloves, minced
pinch of dried oregano
1 tsp apple cider vinegar
¼ c raisins

1. Although I remove the stems from most leafy greens, I leave them intact here. (If you use collards or kale, you'll want to cut away the stems.) Coarsely chop well-rinsed chard, and set aside.

2. Line a large pot or skillet with a thin layer of water.

3. Add garlic, oregano, and vinegar and bring to a boil, sautéing garlic over high heat for a minute.

4. Add raisins and cook for another minute, then add chard. Use tongs or a spatula to stir chard around so it cooks down and incorporates with the other ingredients.

5. Once chard is softer and brighter in color, turn off heat and mix everything well.

6. Season with salt and pepper and serve.

NUTRITIONAL INFORMATION 👁 **78** Calories, **0.3g** Fat, **19.1g** Carbohydrates, **2g** Fiber, **11.6g** Sugars, **2.2g** Protein

Andrea's Tofu Fries F G $

Serves 4 | The first time my friend Andrea told me about these tofu fries I thought she was crazy. Tofu as a French fry? While they are not exactly the same as golden deep-fried potatoes, they're close and really addictive. Plus they're full of protein!

1 lb extra-firm tofu
choice of seasonings such as Cajun Seasoning (pg. 277), salt and pepper, or garlic salt

1. Preheat your toaster oven or conventional oven using the broil setting.
2. Grease a cookie sheet (or the toaster oven tray) or line with parchment paper and set aside.
3. Cut tofu into strips the size of French fries.
4. Place "fries" on your prepared sheet and spritz with oil spray. Sprinkle generously with your choice of seasoning, then shake the tray so the "fries" rotate over. Spritz again and sprinkle with more seasoning.
5. Broil for 20 minutes, or until crisp.

CHEF'S NOTE: For best results, drain tofu, freeze it in a zippered plastic bag overnight and then let it thaw in the fridge for a few hours (while you're at work, for example) before making these fries.

NUTRITIONAL INFORMATION **43** Calories, **0.8g** Fat, **1.1g** Carbohydrates, **0g** Fiber, **0g** Sugars, **7.9g** Protein

Cajun Potato Salad

Serves 6 | This New Orleans–inspired potato salad uses the Creamy Cajun Mustard as its base. It's creamy, tangy, and a little spicy. Be sure to serve it as a side with Oyster Po'Boys (pg. 76)!

1 lb red potatoes, diced
Creamy Cajun Mustard
    (pg. 269)
2 tbsp chopped chives
vegan bacon bits
    (optional)
paprika or Cajun
    Seasoning (pg. 277)
    for garnish

1. Bring a large pot of water to a boil.
2. Add potatoes and cook until fork-tender, about 5 minutes.
3. Immediately rinse with cold water and allow to completely cool.
4. Transfer to a mixing bowl and stir in Creamy Cajun Mustard until all the potatoes are well coated.
5. Toss a few times with chives to ensure even distribution and sprinkle generously with bacon bits, if using.
6. Garnish with a heavy dash of paprika or Cajun Seasoning, cover and chill, until just before serving, at least 1 hour.

CHEF'S NOTE: The dark-green parts of green onions may be substituted for the chives.

NUTRITIONAL INFORMATION ⬥ 61 Calories, 0.4g Fat, 12.9g Carbohydrates, 1.6g Fiber, 1.2g Sugars, 2.1g Protein

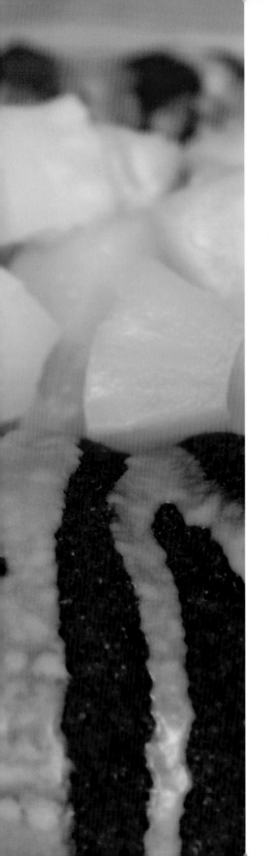

Desserts

Butter Bean Cookies

Makes 2 dozen | If I can turn black beans into brownies, why can't I turn butter beans into chocolate chip cookies? These are the best low-fat and protein-packed cookies you'll ever eat!

1 c rolled oats, divided
1 c whole-wheat pastry
   flour
1 tsp baking powder
½ tsp baking soda
pinch of salt
¼ tsp ground cinnamon
dash of ground
   cardamom (optional)
1 15-oz can white beans,
   drained and unrinsed
   but all liquids reserved
¼ c unsweetened
   applesauce
½ c raw sugar
½ tsp vanilla extract
½ c vegan chocolate chips

> **CHEF'S NOTE:**
> Any white beans
> (butter beans, navy
> beans, cannellini
> beans, etc.) can be
> used in this recipe.

1. Preheat oven to 350°F. Grease a large cookie sheet or line with parchment paper and set aside.

2. Transfer ¾ cup of the oats to a food processor or blender, and pulse, about 15 times, until crumbly but not powdery or flourlike.

3. Transfer to a mixing bowl and combine with flour, baking powder, baking soda, salt, cinnamon, and a dash of cardamom, if using. Whisk to incorporate everything and set aside.

4. Transfer ½ cup of beans (unrinsed) to a food processor or blender and add applesauce, sugar, vanilla extract, and 1 tablespoon of the reserved bean liquid. Blend until smooth. Pour wet mixture into dry mixture and stir about 10 times.

5. Add chocolate chips, remaining ¼ cup of oats, and the rest of the reserved bean liquid, stirring until well combined. If the mixture is too wet, add more oats. If it's too dry, add a little water.

6. Drop tablespoons of batter onto the cookie sheet, leaving an inch of room between them, and flatten them slightly so they look more like cookies than balls.

7. Bake for 15 minutes, or until the edges are just turning light brown and middles are firm (the bottoms should also be golden brown). The cookies firm a bit more as they cool.

NUTRITIONAL INFORMATION (1 COOKIE) 👁 61 Calories, **0.7g** Fat, **12.4g** Carbohydrates, **1.4g** Fiber, **5.2g** Sugars, **1.3g** Protein

SXM Strudel ㉚ Ⓕ Ⓢ $ ①

Serves 1 | Top Carrot, a veg-friendly cafe in St. Maarten, makes apple strudel out of tortillas. At first I thought it was strange—an apple burrito? An apple roll-up? But once I ate one, I realized it was pure genius. Forget the fuss of puff pastry!

1 apple, cored and thinly
    sliced
1 tbsp brown sugar
 dash of ground cinnamon
1 whole-wheat tortilla

CHEF'S NOTE:
For a more decadent treat, combine ½ cup of powdered sugar with 1 tsp of nondairy milk as needed to form a thick glaze. Dip a fork into the glaze and drizzle it over the warm strudel.

1. Preheat oven to 350°F. Line a baking sheet with parchment paper, and set aside.

2. Toss the apples in a mixing bowl with sugar and several dashes of cinnamon, until apple slices are well coated.

3. If you want that ooey-gooey, apple-pie filling, you'll need to pan-fry the apples while your oven preheats (otherwise put raw apples straight in the tortilla as directed below). Line a skillet with a thin layer of water and sauté apples over high heat until they start to soften and the water has cooked off, about 4 minutes.

4. Turn off heat and quickly microwave your tortilla for 5 to 15 seconds, so that it's soft and pliable (perhaps longer if you kept it in the fridge, but it shouldn't be longer than 20 or 30 seconds).

5. Spoon the apples into the center of the tortilla, leaving a few slices aside, then roll up the tortilla like a burrito.

6. Place it crease side down on the baking sheet with a few place apple slices over top. Bake for 10 to 15 minutes, until golden and crispy, but not burned, or bake for less time if you still want it to be soft.

NUTRITIONAL INFORMATION

SXM STRUDEL (WITH TORTILLA) 182 Calories, 1g Fat, 44.9g Carbohydrates, 6g Fiber, 27.9g Sugars, 1.9g Protein

SXM STRUDEL (WITHOUT TORTILLA) 130 Calories, 0.3g Fat, 34.2g Carbohydrates, 4.5g Fiber, 27.7g Sugars, 0.5g Protein

Soft Molasses Cookies

Makes 14 | These cookies are so soft and fluffy they could float away on a cloud.

1 c oat flour

1 tbsp cornstarch

½ to 1 tsp baking soda
(see Chef's Note)

pinch of salt

½ tsp ground cinnamon

¼ tsp ground ginger

⅛ tsp allspice, nutmeg, or
ground cloves

¼ c mashed navy beans

¼ c molasses

2 tbsp unsweetened
applesauce

2 tbsp brown or raw
sugar (optional)

1. To make oat flour, whiz instant or rolled oats in your blender until they reach a flourlike consistency.

2. Mix 1 cup of oat flour, cornstarch, baking soda, salt, and spices together in a mixing bowl until well combined.

3. Add remaining ingredients and stir until just combined.

4. Set batter aside to rest while oven heats to 350°F.

5. Grease a cookie sheet or line with parchment paper.

6. Drop 14 spoonfuls of batter onto the cookie sheet.

7. Bake for 10 to 15 minutes, or until cookies are firm to the touch.

> **CHEF'S NOTE:** For a less puffy and denser cookie, use only ½ teaspoon of baking soda. Use the full teaspoon for very soft and pillow-like cookies.

NUTRITIONAL INFORMATION (1 COOKIE) **47** Calories, **0.7g** Fat, **9.9g** Carbohydrates, **0.8g** Fiber, **3.5g** Sugars, **0.9g** Protein

Chai-Oat Cookies ③⓪ Ⓖ Ⓢ Ⓢ

Makes 10 | I've borrowed the texture and shape from my husband's favorite cookies—Mexican wedding cookies, and added chai flavoring to these delicious gluten-free treats! Any white bean such as navy, butter, or cannellini beans may be used here (drain, but do not rinse!).

1 c oat flour
½ c white beans, drained
1 very ripe banana
½ tsp ground cinnamon
½ tsp ground cardamom
½ tsp ground ginger
¼ tsp ground cloves
¼ tsp garam masala
¼ tsp salt
¼ c light brown or raw
   sugar (optional)
¼ c instant oats
½ c powdered sugar, for
   rolling

1. To make oat flour, whiz instant or rolled oats in your blender until they reach a flourlike consistency.

2. Measure 1 cup of oat flour and set aside. In a mixing bowl, mash beans and banana with a fork to the consistency of refried beans.

3. Stir in spices, salt, and sugar, and mix well.

4. Using an electric mixer, beat in oat flour.

5. Add ¼ cup of instant oats, stirring to combine and set batter aside to rest.

6. Preheat oven to 350°F.

7. Grease a cookie sheet or line with parchment paper and set aside.

8. Pick off walnut-sized portions of the batter and roll into balls, stopping to wash hands periodically so the batter doesn't stick.

9. Bake for 10 to 12 minutes, until firm and the bottoms are slightly golden.

10. Let cool for a few minutes, then spritz lightly with oil spray and rolls balls in powdered sugar.

NUTRITIONAL INFORMATION (1 COOKIE) 🥄 **90** Calories, **1.2g** Fat, **17g** Carbohydrates, **3.9g** Fiber, **2.6g** Sugars, **3.8g** Protein

Chickpea Puffs Ⓖ Ⓢ $

Serves 2 | My superstar assistant, Andrea Dermos, created this recipe—they're like Cocoa Puffs, except they're made with chickpeas!

½ 15-oz can chickpeas, drained and rinsed
1 tbsp unsweetened cocoa
1 tbsp vanilla extract
1 tsp raw sugar
1 tbsp vegan chocolate chips

1. Preheat oven to 350°F.
2. Grease a cookie sheet or line with parchment paper and set aside.
3. Spritz a tiny bit of cooking spray on the chickpeas in a plastic reusable container. (You don't need much spray since the chickpeas are already somewhat wet.)
4. Add cocoa, vanilla, and raw sugar on top and set aside.
5. Melt chocolate by heating it for a few seconds in the microwave and then drizzle over the chickpeas. Put the lid on the container and shake it around so everything is well coated.
6. Transfer chickpeas to your cookie sheet and bake for 30 minutes, or until they are crunchy.

CHEF'S NOTE: For a peanut butter cup flavor, heat a dab of peanut butter with the chocolate chips, or add ½ to 1 teaspoon of peanut flour.

NUTRITIONAL INFORMATION (½ C) **179** Calories, **3g** Fat, **30g** Carbohydrates, **5.3g** Fiber, **5.7g** Sugars, **5.8g** Protein

Apple Fritter Cups

Makes 1 dozen | As my friend Sheree` says, "These treats just jump right in to your mouth and make you dance!"

1½ c chopped apple
  (skin optional)
1 tsp cinnamon, divided
¼ c light brown or raw
  sugar
1 c nondairy milk
1 tsp apple cider vinegar
2 c whole-wheat pastry
  flour
½ tsp salt
½ tsp baking powder
½ tsp baking soda
dash of ground nutmeg or
  ground ginger
2 tsp vanilla extract
Basic Glaze (pg. 62)

1. Preheat oven to 350°F.
2. Fill muffin tin with paper liners and set aside.
3. Toss 1 cup of apple slices with a few dashes of cinnamon and a little brown sugar until well coated and set aside. (This is the topping.)
4. In a small bowl, whisk nondairy milk with vinegar and set aside.
5. In a large bowl, whisk flour, salt, baking powder, baking soda, and ½ to ¾ teaspoon of cinnamon (your choice), plus a dash of nutmeg or ginger, and stir to combine. Whisk in sugar, then pour in milk mixture. Add vanilla and remaining ½ cup of apples and stir to combine.
6. Spoon into muffin cups, filling just a tad more than halfway. Add sugar-cinnamon apple topping on each.
7. Bake 15 to 25 minutes, until a toothpick inserted in the center comes out clean.
8. Meanwhile, make Basic Glaze, substituting 1 teaspoon of liquid with 1 teaspoon of pure maple syrup (optional).
9. Drizzle warm fritters with glaze.

CHEF'S NOTE:
Once the fritters cool completely, the liners will peel off. If you plan to eat them warm, lightly spray the inside of the liner with oil spray to prevent sticking.

NUTRITIONAL INFORMATION (1 FRITTER, WITHOUT GLAZE) **102** Calories, **0.4g** Fat, **20.9g** Carbohydrates, **2.4g** Fiber, **5.5g** Sugars, **2.7g** Protein

Tortuga Rum Cake

Serves 9 | Pictured opposite and on pg. 238 | I don't know what it is about the Caribbean that gets you hooked on rum. Before I moved to St. Maarten I loathed rum, and now I'm trying to slip it into everything. Hmm.... Anyway, this rum cake is so rich and flavorful no one will believe it's made with whole grains and no added fat. Use a very dark rum such as Myers's Rum for maximum flavor.

1 c oat flour
1 c white whole-wheat flour
1 tsp baking powder
½ tsp baking soda
½ tsp salt
1 tsp ground cinnamon
⅔ c light brown sugar
¼ c molasses
¼ c unsweetened
    applesauce
1 tsp vanilla extract
½ c dark rum
½ c nondairy milk

ICING
1 c powdered sugar
1 tsp rum
1 tbsp tangerine or
    orange zest
2 tsp nondairy milk

1. Preheat oven to 350°F.
2. Grease a cake pan and set aside.
3. To make oat flour, whiz instant or rolled oats in your blender until it reaches a flour-like consistency.
4. In a medium mixing bowl, combine 1 cup of oat flour with wheat flour, baking powder, baking soda, salt, spices, and sugar.
5. Add wet ingredients in order, then stir to combine.
6. Pour into prepared pan and bake for 25 to 40 minutes, until a toothpick inserted in the middle comes out clean. (Usually it takes about 35 minutes.)
7. Meanwhile, make icing. In a small bowl, whisk powdered sugar with rum, zest, and nondairy milk as necessary until a runny glaze forms.
8. Spoon the icing over the warm cake and let run down the sides.

NUTRITIONAL INFORMATION

TORTUGA RUM CAKE, WITH ICING — **244** Calories, **1.2g** Fat, **49.2g** Carbohydrates, **2.6g** Fiber, **30.6g** Sugars, **3.7g** Protein

TORTUGA RUM CAKE, WITHOUT ICING — **190** Calories, **1.2g** Fat, **35.7g** Carbohydrates, **2.6g** Fiber, **17.4g** Sugars, **3.6g** Protein

ICING (1 TBSP) — **61** Calories, **0g** Fat, **15.2g** Carbohydrates, **0g** Fiber, **14.9g** Sugars, **0.1g** Protein

Oatmeal Chews ㉚ Ⓕ Ⓖ Ⓢ ⑤

Makes 15 | These ultra-healthy cookies are made with zero added sugars! I like to take them with me on long hikes and bike rides for a boost of energy.

2 small bananas (very ripe)
¼ c soaked raisins
¼ c unsweetened
   applesauce
1 tsp vanilla extract
dash of ground cinnamon
1¼ c instant oats

CHEF'S NOTE:
Bake less time for a
soft and chewy cookie
and bake longer for a
harder cookie.

1. Combine all ingredients except oats in a blender and puree until smooth. A few raisin bits are okay, but you don't want pieces or chunks.

2. Combine mixture with oats in a mixing bowl until well combined.

3. Let batter rest for a minimum of 5 minutes while you preheat your oven to 350°F.

4. Grease cookie sheet or line with parchment paper.

5. Drop tablespoonfuls of the batter onto the cookie sheet and flatten slightly with your hands. Use your fingers to shape into a circular cookie shape. Repeat 15 times or until no batter is left.

6. Bake for 10 to 14 minutes, or until the cookies feel firm to the touch and are a deep golden color.

7. Let stand for a minute before transferring to a wire rack to cool (they firm as they cool).

CHEF'S NOTE: If you don't have a strong blender, you'll need to soak the raisins in water overnight, or in hot water for 10 minutes, to get them to blend properly. This process also makes the cookies a tad sweeter.

NUTRITIONAL INFORMATION (1 COOKIE) 🍪 **36** Calories, **0.3g** Fat, **7.8g** Carbohydrates, **0.8g** Fiber, **3.6g** Sugars, **0.7g** Protein

Natala's Chocolate-Cherry Shake

Serves 2 | Natala's story of how adopting a plant-based diet saved her life is incredible and all-inspiring. She blogs about her experiences and helps others heal with food through her website, Veganhope.com. This is Natala's recipe and it's so rich and chocolatey, you'll never believe it has two servings of greens slipped in!

1 ripe frozen banana

1 c frozen cherries

2 c fresh spinach

1 c nondairy milk or water

2 tbsp unsweetened cocoa

1 tbsp vegan chocolate chips (optional)

1 cherry for garnish (optional)

1 Blend all ingredients (except the optional chocolate chips and cherry garnish) until smooth, adding more liquid as necessary.

2 Garnish with chocolate chips and a cherry.

CHEF'S NOTE: Natala likes to use unsweetened dark carob or carob powder here since some vegan chocolates contain sugar and other additives, but I used vegan chocolate chips for convenience. You can find carob and carob powder at health food stores.

NUTRITIONAL INFORMATION

NATALA'S CHOCOLATE-CHERRY SHAKE, WITH NONDAIRY MILK
149 Calories, **1.5g** Fat, **32.1g** Carbohydrates, **5.2g** Fiber, **20.7g** Sugars, **7.4g** Protein

NATALA'S CHOCOLATE-CHERRY SHAKE, WITH WATER **107** Calories, **1.4g** Fat, **26g** Carbohydrates, **5.2g** Fiber, **14.4g** Sugars. **3.3g** Protein

Chocolate Mug Cake 30 Ⓢ $ ❶

Serves 1 | Chocolate cake? Check. Single serving? Check. Made nearly instantly? Oh yeah! This whole-wheat chocolate cake goes from flour to in your mouth in under 5 minutes.

4 tbsp white whole-wheat
    flour
2 tbsp brown sugar
2 tbsp unsweetened cocoa
¼ tsp baking powder
dash of ground cinnamon
¼ c unsweetened
    applesauce
3 tbsp nondairy milk
1 to 2 drops vanilla extract
2 to 3 tbsp vegan
    chocolate chips

❶ In a small bowl, whisk flour, sugar, cocoa, baking powder, and cinnamon together; set aside. For a really sweet cake, add more sugar.

❷ In another small bowl, whisk ¼ cup of applesauce, nondairy milk, and vanilla extract together.

❸ Pour wet into dry, then add chips, stirring to combine.

❹ Add another 1 to 2 tablespoons of applesauce, until the batter is wet and resembles regular cake batter.

❺ Pour batter into a coffee cup, and microwave for three minutes (at 1,000 watts).

VARIATION

Chocolate-Banana Mug Cake 30 Ⓢ $ ❶ 🍃 Reduce applesauce to 3 tablespoons. Combine nondairy milk, 1 small very ripe banana, 3 tablespoons of applesauce, and vanilla in a blender and whiz until smooth and creamy. Mix into flour mixture with chips and cook as directed.

NUTRITIONAL INFORMATION

CHOCOLATE MUG CAKE 🍃 **276** Calories, **4.1g** Fat, **59.3g** Carbohydrates, **7.8g** Fiber, **31.6g** Sugars, **8.3g** Protein

CHOCOLATE-BANANA MUG CAKE 🍃 **264** Calories, **2.2g** Fat, **61.4g** Carbohydrates, **8.3g** Fiber, **30.2g** Sugars, **8.2g** Protein

Pineapple Sponge Cake Ⓕ Ⓢ Ⓢ

Serves 9 | I'm always getting requests for sugar-free desserts, and decided to try my hand at it here. All the sweetness in this cake comes from pineapple juice, making this a wet cake, sometimes called sponge cake or pudding cake.

1 15-oz can pineapple rings (in 100% juice)
1 c whole-wheat pastry flour
1 tsp baking powder
½ tsp baking soda
pinch of salt
3 dashes of ground ginger
1 tsp vanilla extract
orange zest (optional)
extra juice for serving

CHEF'S NOTE:
Make sure the pineapple rings you buy come in 100% juice and not syrup.

1. Preheat oven to 350°F. Grease an 8- or 9-inch cake pan and set aside.
2. Drain pineapple juice into a small bowl and set aside.
3. In a mixing bowl, whisk flour, baking powder, baking soda, salt, and a few dashes of ground ginger together. Add vanilla extract and zest (if using) and set aside.
4. Chop pineapple rings really well, or send through your blender until they have the consistency of crushed, minced pineapple (but not puree).
5. Mix pineapple into flour mixture, stirring to combine.
6. Add pineapple juice, starting with ¼ cup and then adding a tablespoon at a time, until the batter is just combined and wet (about 6 tablespoons total).
7. Transfer to pan and bake for approximately 20 minutes.
8. Pour leftover juice, plus additional juice, over the top immediately before serving. You want the cake to be wet and nearly falling apart.

CHEF'S NOTE: If you prefer a sweeter dessert, ¼ to ½ cup of raw sugar can be added.

NUTRITIONAL INFORMATION 🥄 **74** Calories, **0.2g** Fat, **15.9g** Carbohydrates, **1.7g** Fiber, **5.1g** Sugars, **1.3g** Protein

Fried Bananas 30 F G S $

Serves 2 | I'm in love with these pan-fried bananas. They remind me of fried plantains you can find in the Caribbean, except they're a whole lot healthier and you don't have to wait 4 weeks for the plantains to ripen.

2 large bananas

CHEF'S NOTE:
You want firm bananas that are not overly ripe. A little green on the ends is ideal.

1. Slice peeled bananas into 1-inch chunks, then slice each chunk in half lengthwise (down the center of the banana).

2. Heat a nonstick skillet over high heat. You'll know it's ready when a drop of water sizzles.

3. Divide banana chunks in half, setting half aside.

4. Place the slimy insides face down on the skillet, one at a time, in a row. It's important to remember the order because as soon as you finish putting the last piece down, it's time to flip the first one. When they've all been flipped once, remove one by one and set aside.

5. Clean out skillet and reheat if necessary. Repeat with remaining banana pieces.

CHEF'S NOTE: I like to sprinkle these with a little cinnamon and powdered sugar for a healthy dessert.

NUTRITIONAL INFORMATION 🍌 **121** Calories, **0.5g** Fat, **31.1g** Carbohydrates, **3.5g** Fiber, **16.6g** Sugars, **1.5g** Protein

Fudge Dip 30 F G S $

Makes 2 cups | Oh, fudge! This dip is so rich you won't believe it's made from beans. Serve with apple and pear slices or smear it into a tortilla, top with banana slices, and roll up. Yum!

1 15-oz can white beans, drained and rinsed
¼ c unsweetened cocoa
2 tbsp agave nectar
nondairy milk

CHEF'S NOTE: Any white beans, such as navy, cannellini, or butter beans may be used here.

1 Blend beans with ¼ cup of cocoa and 2 tablespoons of agave nectar in a strong blender or food processor until well combined, adding a splash of nondairy milk as necessary to achieve a creamed consistency.

2 Taste, then add 1 tablespoon of cocoa at a time until you're satisfied with the richness. I like it at 6 tablespoons but my dark-chocolate-loving testers went up to 8 tablespoons (½ cup total). You may also need to add another 1 tablespoon of agave nectar for your tastes. The end result should be the consistency of icing, the kind you buy at the store in a tub.

VARIATIONS

Peanut Butter Fudge Dip 30 G S $ 🥜 For an even richer dip, add peanut butter to taste, 1 tablespoon at a time; or for a low-fat option, use peanut flour.

CHEF'S NOTE: For my sweetener-free friends, you can use ⅓ to ½ cup of soaked dates instead of agave nectar: just blend them with ¼ cup of nondairy milk or water first (it will form a paste) and add with beans and cocoa.

NUTRITIONAL INFORMATION (2 TBSP) 🥜 **80** Calories, **0.6g** Fat, **16.7g** Carbohydrates, **3.6g** Fiber, **4.5g** Sugars, **4.5g** Protein

Carrot Cake Rice Pudding ⓖ ⓢ ⓧ $

Serves 2 | Anytime I have leftover brown rice at dinner I make this pudding for breakfast the following morning. It's traditionally served as a chilled dessert (called gajar ki kheer) in Pakistan, but I find it's a filling breakfast, plus it's a great way to start the day, with fruits, vegetables, and whole foods.

1 c nondairy milk
1 tbsp cornstarch
1 c grated carrots
⅓ c raisins
1 c cooked brown rice
ground cardamom, to taste
raw sugar, agave nectar,
    maple syrup, or other
    sweetener (optional)
dash of ground cinnamon
    for garnish

CHEF'S NOTE:
This dish is traditionally sweetened with sugar, but I find it's sweet enough with the raisins. And, you can add any sweetener you like to taste (maple syrup is my favorite).

1. Whisk nondairy milk with cornstarch, and set aside.

2. Send your carrots through a food processor or blender, or grate manually with a cheese grater, and set aside.

3. Line a medium pot with a thin layer of water. Bring to a boil and add carrots and raisins, cooking for a minute or so until the carrots are soft and fragrant and the raisins look softer and a little more plump. Add nondairy milk mixture and rice, stirring to combine.

4. Bring to a boil, then reduce heat to low. Continue to cook, stirring frequently, until it thickens, about 4 minutes.

5. Add a few dashes of cardamom, stirring to incorporate. I find some cardamom is more potent than others, so it's good to add it to taste. You want to add enough so there is a nice cardamom aroma, but not so much it overpowers. Most traditional recipes call for ¾ to 1 teaspoon.

6. Turn off heat and allow the pudding to cool completely before storing it in the fridge (preferably in a glass bowl with plastic wrap, but airtight containers also work). Chill overnight, or for several hours, until it's cool and creamy.

NUTRITIONAL INFORMATION 🥄 **266** Calories, **1.2g** Fat, **58.3g** Carbohydrates, **3.6g** Fiber, **23.2g** Sugars, **7.8g** Protein

Banana Pudding 30 F G S 1

Serves 1 | I love to eat this pudding as a cool afternoon snack on a hot day or as a light dessert. It reminds me of a pudding my mom used to make with Nilla Wafers, and the chocolate pudding variation (below) tastes like icing when you use very ripe bananas. I dare say these puddings will ensure you always have cooked quinoa on hand and stored in your fridge!

1 cold banana
3 tbsp nondairy milk
2 tbsp cooked quinoa
½ tsp agave nectar
  (optional)
dash of cinnamon or
  pumpkin pie spice

1 Combine all ingredients in a blender and puree until smooth and thick.

2 Taste, add agave nectar if desired, and serve immediately. Bananas turn brown as they oxidize, so it's best to make this pudding shortly before eating it or your pudding might not look very appetizing.

VARIATION

Chocolate Banana Pudding 30 G S 1 ✎ Add 1 tablespoon of unsweetened cocoa and omit spices.

> **CHEF'S NOTE:** If you don't have a strong blender, use a food processor or overcook the quinoa, meaning add more water than called for when cooking, so it's a bit waterlogged and softer.

NUTRITIONAL INFORMATION

BANANA PUDDING ✎ **151** Calories, **1.5g** Fat, **35.4g** Carbohydrates, **5.2g** Fiber, **16.9** Sugars. **4.6g** Protein

CHOCOLATE BANANA PUDDING ✎ **162** Calories, **1.4g** Fat, **38.3g** Carbohydrates, **5g** Fiber, **19.7g** Sugars, **4.5g** Protein

Condiments & Spice Blends

Chipotle Mayo 30 F G $

Makes ~3 tbsp | I love this mayo and it's my go-to condiment anytime I feel like my sandwich needs a little something extra. I designed it to complement the Pinto Burgers (pg. 86), but it can be used as a condiment however you wish.

¼ to ½ tsp chipotle powder
3 tbsp Vegan Mayo
    (pg. 272)
1 tsp liquid smoke
⅛ tsp paprika

1. In a small bowl, whisk all ingredients together, starting with ¼ teaspoon of chipotle.

2. Taste, adding another ¼ teaspoon of chipotle (recommended) if desired, plus salt and pepper to taste.

> CHEF'S NOTE: For a really spicy kick, add a little hot sauce or Asian hot sauce like Sriracha.

NUTRITIONAL INFORMATION (1 TBSP) 🥄 **10** Calories, **0.1g** Fat, **1.5g** Carbohydrates, **0g** Fiber, **1.2g** Sugars, **0.9g** Protein

Smoky Cajun Mayo

Makes ¼ cup | Perhaps my favorite condiment, this slightly spicy and smoky mayo really adds oomph to any sandwich.

¼ cup Vegan Mayo
  (pg. 272)
2 tsp Cajun Seasoning
  (pg. 277)
1 tsp liquid smoke

1 Mix all ingredients together and taste, adding more Cajun Seasoning or liquid smoke as desired.

Masala Mayo

Makes 3 tbsp | *Pictured on pg. 264* | A lovely Indian-spiced mayo designed for the Masala Burgers (pg. 83), but it's also a great condiment on any sandwich that could use a splash of bold flavor.

2 tbsp ketchup
1 tbsp Vegan Mayo
  (pg. 272)
½ tsp yellow mustard
¼ tsp garam masala
¼ tsp coriander
¼ + ⅛ tsp ground cumin
drop of agave nectar
  (optional)

1 Mix all ingredients together.

2 Taste, adding another ¼ teaspoon of garam masala if necessary (some blends are more potent than others) and agave nectar to taste if needed.

NUTRITIONAL INFORMATION

SMOKY CAJUN MAYO (1 TBSP) ⬥ **9** Calories, **0g** Fat, **1.2g** Carbohydrates, **1.2g** Sugars, **0g** Fiber, **0.9g** Protein

MASALA MAYO (1 TBSP) ⬥ **9** Calories, **0g** Fat, **1.2g** Carbohydrates, **1.2g** Sugars, **0g** Fiber, **0.9g** Protein

"Honey" Mustard

Makes 2 tbsp | *Pictured opposite* | This honey mustard has a slight kick to it. It's great as a dipping sauce, condiment, or salad dressing. I keep a big batch of it in a small airtight container in my fridge, but it takes seconds to whip up when you need it.

1 tbsp Dijon mustard
1 tbsp raw agave nectar
hot sauce, to taste
dash of ground ginger

1. In a small bowl, whisk Dijon and agave nectar together.
2. Add a few drops of hot sauce (to your taste) plus a dash or two of ground ginger; mix again.
3. Taste, adjusting sugar, mustard, or hot sauce as needed.

Creamy Cajun Mustard

Makes ⅓ cup | You can find commercial creamy Cajun mustards in Louisiana, but I prefer making it myself so it's always available and I can adjust the heat to my preferences.

3 tbsp Dijon mustard
½ tsp Vegan
    Worcestershire Sauce
    (pg. 302)
½ tsp hot sauce
1 tsp molasses
1 tbsp Vegan Mayo
    (pg. 272)
¼ tsp Cajun Seasoning
    (pg. 277)

1. Combine all ingredients, adding more Cajun Seasoning if you like. I scaled it down here since some blends are hotter than others.
2. If your Dijon is too strong, you can add a bit more mayo to tone it down. You can also add a touch more molasses for a sweeter mustard.

NUTRITIONAL INFORMATION

"HONEY" MUSTARD (1 TBSP) 38 Calories, 0.3g Fat, 9.2g Carbohydrates, 0g Fiber, 8.7g Sugars, 0.4g Protein

CREAMY CAJUN MUSTARD (1 TBSP) 12 Calories, 0.4g Fat, 1.8g Carbohydrates, 0g Fiber, 1.1g Sugars, 0.6g Protein

Lime Crème

Makes ¼ cup | *Pictured opposite* | This recipe is compliments of my friend Jane who rules at all things lime-flavored.

¼ c Sour Cream (pg. 274)
1 tsp chili powder
½ tsp lime zest
¼ tsp salt

1. Mix all ingredients until well-combined.
2. Taste, adjusting chili powder as needed or desired.
3. Chill for 5 minutes before using, giving the flavors a chance to blend.

Rémoulade

Makes ¼ cup | Invented in France, this creamy condiment is a popular accoutrement to seafood, so it goes perfectly with the "Crab" Cakes (pg. 187).

1 tbsp Vegan Mayo
   (pg. 272)
1 tbsp plus ¼ tsp ketchup
1 tbsp dill relish
¼ tsp yellow mustard
¼ tsp Old Bay seasoning
juice of 1 lemon wedge
hot sauce, to taste

1. Mix all ingredients together, including a few drops of hot sauce.
2. Taste, adding more Old Bay seasoning or hot sauce as desired. If your relish isn't very salty, you might want to add a pinch of sea salt.

CHEF'S NOTE: Minced dill pickle may be substituted for the relish.

NUTRITIONAL INFORMATION

LIME CRÈME (1 TBSP) ⏺ 11 Calories, 0.1g Fat, 1.6g Carbohydrates, 0g Fiber, 1.2g Sugars, 1g Protein

RÉMOULADE (1 TBSP) ⏺ 8 Calories, 0g Fat, 1.6g Carbohydrates, 0g Fiber, 1.5g Sugars, 0.3g Protein

Vegan Mayo

Makes 1 cup | Nasoya makes a fat-free vegan mayonnaise, and some generic low-fat mayos are accidentally vegan. Here is my easy and inexpensive recipe for making your own low-fat vegan mayo at home.

1 12.3-oz pkg Mori-Nu tofu
2 to 3 tbsp Dijon mustard
2 tsp distilled white
   vinegar
lemon juice, to taste
agave nectar, to taste

1. In a blender or small food processor, blend tofu with Dijon and vinegar until smooth and creamy.

2. Add a few drops of lemon juice and a few drops of agave nectar and blend again.

3. Taste and add more lemon, agave nectar, or Dijon as needed or desired. Chill until you're ready to use.

> **CHEF'S NOTE:** In a pinch or for soy-free, substitute plain (preferably unsweetened) vegan yogurt.

NUTRITIONAL INFORMATION (1 TBSP) **10** Calories, **0.2g** Fat, **0.3g** Carbohydrates, **0g** Sugar, **0g** Fiber, **1.6g** Protein

Poultry Seasoning Mix ③⓪ Ⓕ Ⓖ Ⓢ $

Makes ¼ cup | This savory herb mixture is my favorite seasoning. You can substitute store-bought poultry blends for convenience; just be sure it's not powdered. The consistency should be like dried basil. In a pinch, Italian seasoning may be substituted.

1 tbsp dried rosemary

1 tbsp dried thyme

1 tbsp rubbed sage (not powdered)

1 tbsp dried marjoram or oregano

1 tbsp dried parsley or basil

1. Grind herbs together in a mortar and pestle until coarse like the consistency of sea salt, but not powdered.

2. Store in an airtight container.

> **CHEF'S NOTE:** If you can find granulated (not powdered) poultry seasoning that isn't a rub, feel free to use it instead for convenience instead of blending your own. I like Cost Plus World Market's generic brand.

NUTRITIONAL INFORMATION (1 TBSP) 🥄 **10** Calories, **0.4g** Fat, **2.0g** Carbohydrates, **1.3g** Fiber, **0g** Sugar, **0.3g** Protein

Cajun Seasoning

Makes ½ cup | Commercial Cajun seasoning blends are often inconsistent when it comes to heat. Some brands are hotter than others, and the spices used in each can also vary. For these reasons I prefer blending my own.

2 tbsp sweet paprika
2 tbsp garlic powder (granulated)
1 tbsp cayenne powder
1 tbsp chili powder
1 tbsp pepper
1 tbsp dried oregano or marjoram
1 tbsp onion powder (granulated)
½ tsp ground nutmeg or mace (optional)

1. Combine all spices and herbs thoroughly.
2. Store in an airtight container.

CHEF'S NOTE: If you want to substitute a commercial blend for convenience, I like McCormick's Cajun Seasoning from their Gourmet Collection and Badia's Louisiana Cajun seasoning.

NUTRITIONAL INFORMATION (1 TBSP) 24 Calories, 0.6g Fat, 4.9g Carbohydrates, 1.9g Fiber, 0g Sugar, 1.1g Protein

Caribbean Dressing 30 G S

Serves 4, makes 2 cups | This recipe uses a hefty amount of avocado, making it not-even-kind-of-fat-free. (Sorry!) But I just had to include it in my cookbook. This "salad" is basically a condiment. It's a bit like the Caribbean's pico de gallo and it's a great addition on top of any Caribbean or island-inspired meal.

1 c cubed avocado
1 c cubed papaya
1 to 2 tsp onion flakes
juice of 1 lime

1. Toss the avocado and papaya together and sprinkle generously with onion flakes. Squeeze lime juice over the top until everything is well coated with it.

2. Mix again and chill until serving.

CHEF'S NOTE: The big melon-sized avocados with the smooth, soft, and green outer shell are best here, rather than the smaller (Hass) avocados with a hard and wrinkled dark brown shell. I find the greener avocados have a more mellow flavor (almost a "watered-down" avocado taste) which keeps them from overpowering the sweet papaya.

CHEF'S NOTE: Minced red onion can stand in place for the onion flakes, but I really like the flavoring of onion flakes.

NUTRITIONAL INFORMATION (½ C) **75** Calories, **5.4g** Fat, **7.5g** Carbohydrates, **3.1g** Fiber, **2.6** Sugars, **1g** Protein

Sauces & Gravies

Teriyaki Sauce 30 F G $

Makes 1¼ cups | Traditionally, teriyaki sauce is made from soy sauce, mirin or sake, and sugar, but I like my teriyaki a little more complex, with a dab of ginger, garlic, and heat. This is my basic teriyaki template, which I vary to make marinades or stir-fries. You can add and subtract to it to make your own personalized teriyaki sauce or marinade; for example, add a little orange marmalade (2 tablespoons), pineapple juice, or more sugar for a sweeter teriyaki.

1 c water
¼ c low sodium soy sauce
1 tbsp cornstarch
½ tsp ground ginger
¼ tsp garlic powder
   (granulated)
3 tsp light brown sugar
dash of red pepper flakes
   (optional)

1. In a small saucepan, whisk all ingredients together until well combined.

2. Bring to a boil and, once boiling, turn off heat and move pot away from the heat.

3. Whisk again and taste. If you prefer a stronger flavor (I do), add another tablespoon of low-sodium soy sauce.

CHEF'S NOTE: Tamari may be substituted for the low-sodium soy sauce to make this teriyaki gluten-free. Agave nectar may also be used to taste in place of the sugar.

NUTRITIONAL INFORMATION (2 TBSP) ⟋ **10** Calories; **0g** Fat; **2.3g** Carbohydrates; **0g** Fiber; **1.0g** Sugars, **0.4g** Protein

Enchilada Sauce F G S $

Makes 4 cups | The secret to making authentic enchilada sauce is the addition of cocoa. Once you've had homemade, you'll never buy enchilada sauce in a can again.

2 tbsp white whole-wheat
   or other flour
1 tsp unsweetened cocoa
2 tbsp chili powder
1 tsp dried oregano or
   marjoram
1 tsp ground cumin
½ tsp garlic powder
   (granulated)
2 c vegetable broth,
   divided
1 8-oz can tomato sauce
salt, to taste (optional)

1. Whisk flour, cocoa, and spices together in a medium saucepan without heat. Add ¼ cup of broth and stir into a paste. Slowly whisk in remaining broth plus and additional 1 cup of water.

2. Bring to a boil over medium heat and whisk in tomato sauce. Allow to cook for a few minutes until it thickens slightly to the consistency of tomato soup.

3. Remove from heat and add salt to taste, if necessary.

Quick Mole Sauce 30 F G S $

Makes 2 cups | *Pictured opposite* | Mole sauce was one of those things I always resisted, but when I finally gave it a try at a restaurant, I was hooked! Mole sauce is awesome! This recipe streamlines the authentic recipe, but the taste is spot on. I like to smother baked tofu with it, but it is most commonly used as an alternative to enchilada sauce.

1 16 oz can tomato sauce
¼ c unsweetened cocoa
¼ c raisins
2¼ tsp chili powder
1 tsp onion powder
   (granulated)
½ tsp ground cinnamon
½ tsp dried oregano
½ tsp ground cumin
pinch of red pepper flakes

1. Combine all ingredients together in a blender and whiz until thick and smooth, and no raisin chunks remain (you may need to stop and scrape the sides). Thin out with a little water or broth as desired.

2. Heat gently in a saucepan over low heat until warm.

NUTRITIONAL INFORMATION

ENCHILADA SAUCE (¼ C) **13** Calories, **0.3g** Fat, **2.8g** Carbohydrates, **0.7g** Fiber, **0.8g** Sugars, **0.5g** Protein

QUICK MOLE SAUCE (¼ C) **37** Calories, **8.8g** Carbohydrates, **2.3g** Fiber, **5.2g** Sugars, **1.6g** Protein

Chickpea Gravy 30 F G S $

Makes 1½ cups | This is one of my all-time favorite gravies. It's great with mashed potatoes and greens alike but my favorite way to eat it is on warm whole-wheat pita with chickpeas and cooked greens and garnished with a dash of paprika. (I call that dish "Lebanese pizza.")

1 c vegetable broth
⅓ c chickpea flour
½ tsp onion powder
 (granulated)
¼ tsp garlic powder
 (granulated)
pinch of Italian seasoning
¼ tsp low-sodium soy
 sauce
black pepper, to taste

1 Whisk all ingredients together in a small saucepan including a generous pinch of Italian seasoning and several dashes of black pepper.

2 Heat over medium until the gravy thickens and comes to a boil. Thin out with ⅓ cup of water or additional broth, adding more if necessary to achieve gravy consistency.

CHEF'S NOTE: For a soy-free variation, use salt to taste instead of low-sodium soy sauce.

NUTRITIONAL INFORMATION (¼ C) **39** Calories, **0.7g** Fat, **6.6g** Carbohydrates, **1.8g** Fiber, **1.2g** Sugars, **2.1g** Protein

Sage Gravy

Makes 1½ cups | Good over greens, mashed potatoes, faux chicken—anything really. This is my latest go-to gravy.

½ c vegetable broth
½ c nondairy milk
1 tbsp rubbed sage (not powdered)
2 tbsp nutritional yeast
2 tbsp white whole-wheat flour
¼ tsp garlic powder (granulated)
¼ tsp onion powder (granulated)
¼ tsp liquid smoke
dash of paprika
juice of 1 lemon wedge
pinch of salt
black or white pepper, to taste

1. Whisk all ingredients together in a medium pot, taking care to rub the sage between your fingers to break it down into smaller bits, especially if your brand is a little rustic with bigger leaves and stem pieces (pull out those stems if you can). Squeeze the juice out of your lemon wedge completely, and discard the rind.

2. Bring gravy to a near-boil over high heat but just before it boils, immediately turn off the heat and remove pot to a nonhot burner, stirring it.

3. Taste, adding black or white pepper as desired.

CHEF'S NOTE: Brown rice flour may be substituted for a gluten-free option.

NUTRITIONAL INFORMATION (¼ C) 29 Calories, 0.3g Fat, 4.7g Carbohydrates, 1.2g Fiber, 1.2g Sugars, 2.6g Protein

Everyday Mushroom Gravy

Makes 1 cup | This is a great everyday gravy, meaning it goes with just about anything and can turn a meal from boring to superb. I love it with mashed potatoes, but it's also great on greens, rice, and couscous.

1 c water
2 tbsp low-sodium soy sauce
2 tbsp nutritional yeast, divided
¼ tsp onion powder (granulated)
¼ tsp garlic powder (granulated)
¼ tsp ground ginger
8 oz white or brown mushrooms, sliced
Italian seasoning
½ c nondairy milk
2 tbsp cornstarch
dash of ground nutmeg (optional)
black pepper, to taste
pinch of salt (optional)

1. In a skillet, whisk water with low-sodium soy sauce, 1 tablespoon of nutritional yeast, onion powder, garlic powder, and ground ginger.

2. Bring to a boil and add mushrooms, sprinkling them generously with Italian seasoning (a good 10 shakes).

3. Continue to sauté over medium-high heat until the mushrooms are brown and soft, about 3 minutes. Meanwhile whisk nondairy milk with cornstarch and remaining 1 tablespoon of nutritional yeast. Add a very light dash of nutmeg, if desired.

4. Pour over mushrooms, stirring to combine. Reduce heat to low and continue to cook until thick and gravylike, about 5 minutes.

5. Add black pepper to taste (I like it really peppery, and a few more shakes of Italian seasoning unless you were very generous before. Taste again, adding a pinch of salt if necessary.

6. Set aside for a few minutes before serving to let the flavors merge.

CHEF'S NOTE: For a smoky-flavored gravy, substitute smoked paprika for the nutmeg, and add more to taste.

NUTRITIONAL INFORMATION (¼ C) 60 Calories, 1.4g Fat, 8.9g Carbohydrates, 1.4g Fiber, 5.6g Protein

Miso Gravy

Serves 2, makes ½ cup | *Pictured opposite and on pg. 280* | I love this miso gravy over cooked greens like kale, collards, turnip greens, or chard, but it's also wonderful over mashed potatoes. For a complete meal, serve with a side of roasted or plain chickpeas.

⅔ cup water
1½ tsp yellow miso
½ tsp low-sodium soy sauce
2 tbsp nutritional yeast
1½ tsp cornstarch
hot sauce, to taste
1 to 2 dashes black pepper

1. In a small saucepan, whisk all ingredients together, adding a few drops of hot sauce and a dash or two of black pepper.

2. Taste, adding ¼ to ½ teaspoon more miso if you want a stronger miso flavor. You can also add more hot sauce if desired.

3. Turn heat to medium and once it looks like it's about to boil, reduce heat to medium-low, stirring until it thickens slightly. It should be thicker than water or broth, but not as thick as most gravies.

4. Drench cooked greens or ladle over mashed potatoes.

> **CHEF'S NOTE:** Any light-colored or mellow miso (such as white or red) may be substituted.

NUTRITIONAL INFORMATION (¼ C) **47** Calories, **0.8g** Fat, **6.4g** Carbohydrates, **2.8g** Fiber, **0g** Sugars, **5.2g** Protein

Simple Cheese Sauce 30 F G S $

Makes 1 cup | *Pictured opposite* | I love all the cheese sauces in my first cookbook, *The Happy Herbivore Cookbook*, but wanted to make an easy, "universal" cheese for everyday cooking. Pour it on pasta, nachos, broccoli, or anything that goes well with a cheddary cheese!

1 c nondairy milk
⅓ c nutritional yeast
¼ c tomato sauce
2 tbsp cornstarch
½ tsp onion powder
   (granulated)
½ tsp garlic powder
   (granulated)
¼ tsp ground cumin

1. Whisk all ingredients together in a saucepan and heat over medium-high until thick, stirring constantly.

Taco Sauce 30 F G S $

Serves 5 | *Pictured opposite* | This is my "secret sauce" for tacos and burritos. It really adds a little something extra and it's effortless to make.

¼ c tomato sauce
⅓ c water
1 tsp chili powder
½ tsp cumin
½ tsp oregano
salt and pepper, to taste
hot sauce, to taste
1 tsp ketchup (optional)

1. Whisk ingredients from tomato sauce through oregano together in a small saucepan and cook over low heat for 5 minutes.

2. Taste, adding salt, black pepper, and hot sauce as desired.

3. If the sauce is too acidic, add a little ketchup.

NUTRITIONAL INFORMATION

SIMPLE CHEESE SAUCE (¼ C) 90 Calories, 0.9g Fat, 14.2g Carbohydrates, 3.7g Fiber, 4g Sugars, 8.5g Protein

SIMPLE CHEESE SAUCE (1 TBSP) 4 Calories, 0.1g Fat, 0.7g Carbohydrates, 0g Sugars, 0g Fiber, 0.2g Protein

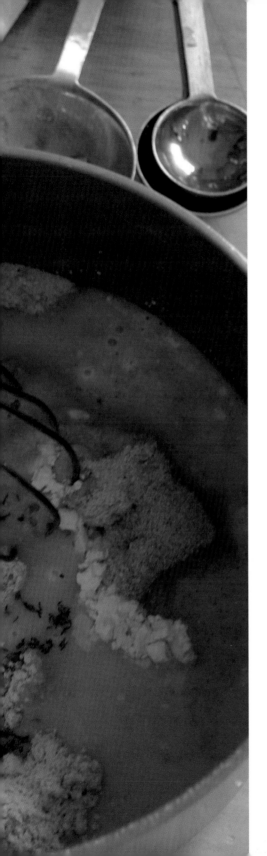

Do-It-Yourself

Instant Applesauce 30 F G S $

Makes 1 cup | *Pictured opposite* | I'm always running out of applesauce in the middle of baking, so I've learned to cheat the system and make my own instantly.

1 McIntosh apple, cored
    and sliced
ground cinnamon, to
    taste (optional)
pumpkin pie spice, to
    taste (optional)

1. Place apple slices in a food processor with 2 tablespoons of water and let the motor run until applesauce is formed, adding 1 to 2 tablespoons more water if needed.

2. Optional: Add cinnamon or pumpkin pie spice for a terrific twist.

3. Store in an airtight container.

Bread Crumbs 30 F S $

Makes approximately 1 cup | Can't find whole-wheat bread crumbs at the store? No problem. All you need is a food processor, a pan, and this duo of steps.

1 slice whole-wheat
    bread

1. Tear bread into equal pieces. Place in a food processor. Allow the motor to run until the bread is shredded and crumbs result.

2. Place in a single layer on a pan and allow to air out and become stale (should be hard and crunchy).

CHEF'S NOTE:
If you're in a hurry, toast crumbs in a conventional oven or toaster oven for a few minutes at 250°F.

NUTRITIONAL INFORMATION

INSTANT APPLESAUCE (¼ C) 👁 **36** Calories, **0.1g** Fat, **9.5g** Carbohydrates, **1.7g** Fiber, **7.2g** Sugars, **0.2g** Protein

BREAD CRUMBS 👁 See your bread's packaging

No-Beef Broth 30 F G $

Makes 1 cup | There are a few commercial mock beef broth bouillon cubes on the market, but I find all of them a little too salty for my taste. This is my DIY version.

1 tbsp low-sodium soy
   sauce
1 tbsp nutritional yeast
½ tsp Vegan
   Worcestershire Sauce
   (pg. 302)
¼ tsp onion powder
   (granulated)
¼ tsp garlic powder
   (granulated)
¼ tsp ground ginger
⅛ tsp pepper
salt, to taste

1. In a medium saucepan, whisk all ingredients together with 1 cup of water until well combined.

2. Bring to a boil and simmer for 1 minute.

3. If you used water and low-sodium soy sauce, you might want to add a little salt.

> **CHEF'S NOTE:** If you use this broth in a soup recipe, add a bay leaf during cooking.

NUTRITIONAL INFORMATION (1 C) 🥄 **27** Calories, **0.2g** Fat, **4.3g** Carbohydrates, **1.1g** Fiber, **0.7g** Sugars, **2.7g** Protein

No-Chicken Broth Powder

Makes approximately 25 servings | Frontier makes a decent vegetarian chicken broth powder, though it contains corn syrup. There are a few commercial mock chicken broth bouillon cubes on the market as well, but I find them a little too salty for my taste. This is my DIY version.

1⅓ c nutritional yeast

2 tbsp onion powder (granulated)

1 tbsp garlic powder (granulated)

1 tsp dried thyme

1 tsp rubbed sage (not powdered)

1 tsp paprika

½ tsp turmeric

¼ tsp celery seed

¼ tsp dried parsley

1. Combine all ingredients and grind with a mortar and pestle into a fine powder.

2. Store in an airtight container, such as a clear glass jar.

> **CHEF'S NOTE:** No-Chicken Broth: Mix 1 tablespoon of the mixture with 1 cup of warm water to yield 1 cup of broth.

NUTRITIONAL INFORMATION (1 TBSP) 12 Calories, **0.1g** Fat, **1.7g** Carbohydrates, **0.7g** Fiber, **1.3g** Protein

Vegetable Broth $

Makes 4 cups | Nothing beats the ease of premade broth or bouillon cubes, but homemade vegetable broth is superior in comparison. It's also a great way to use up veggies that are on their way to expiration. I like to use sweet onions, potatoes, parsnips, turnips, and fresh fennel.

1 onion (any), peeled
1 large carrot
1 celery stalk
3 to 4 garlic cloves, peeled
3 to 5 oz fresh or dried
   herbs (any)
1 to 2 tsp yellow miso
4 whole black peppercorns
1 bay leaf
8 to 10 c water

PLUS ANY THREE OF THE FOLLOWING:

1 small brown potato
2 to 4 small red potatoes
1 c mushrooms
1 bell pepper, seeded
1 medium turnip
1 medium zucchini
1 parsnip
1 leek

1. Transfer onion, carrot, celery, garlic, and your three additional veggie selections to a large pot. If using dried herbs, grab each green one you have on hand and give it a good shake into the pot. Otherwise add fresh dill or any complementary fresh herbs you have.

2. Add 1 to 2 teaspoons of miso, peppercorns, and bay leaf.

3. Add 8 cups of cold water, or 10 cups if your selections are particularly big.

4. Cover and bring to a boil. Reduce heat to low and simmer until the vegetables are falling apart, about 1 hour.

5. Turn off heat and allow to cool to a warm temperature.

6. Use tongs or a spoon to remove bay leaf and vegetables.

7. Grab a cheesecloth or fine strainer and strain liquid into a plastic container.

8. Cool to room temperature, then store in the fridge for up to 3 days. After 3 days, store in freezer in 1-cup measurements.

CHEF'S NOTE: You can omit the miso and add salt to taste for a soy-free vegetable broth.

NUTRITIONAL INFORMATION (1 C) **49** Calories, **0.4g** Fat, **10.6g** Carbohydrates, **2.2g** Fiber, **4.1g** Sugars, **2.2g** Protein

Vegan Worcestershire Sauce

Makes 1 cup | Most commercial Worcestershire sauces contain anchovies, although there are a few vegetarian brands on the market. While nothing beats the ease of bottled sauce, this DIY recipe is allergen-free and very inexpensive to make. Worcestershire sauce is traditionally used as a condiment for meat, and consequently is a great marinade for veggie burgers and acts as a flavoring agent in many meat substitute recipes.

6 tbsp apple cider vinegar
2 tbsp tamari
1 tbsp brown sugar, or
    1 tsp molasses
2 tsp prepared mustard
    (any)
¼ tsp onion powder
    (granulated)
¼ tsp garlic powder
    (granulated)
¼ tsp ground ginger
⅛ tsp ground cinnamon
light dash of cayenne or
    chili powder
light dash of allspice or
    ground cloves
salt (optional)

1. Whisk all ingredients together with ¼ cup of water until well combined.
2. Add salt if desired.
3. Store in an airtight container in the fridge.

CHEF'S NOTE: Yeast extract such as Marmite and Vegemite can be used in place of Worcestershire sauce if Worcestershire sauce is being used an ingredient in something and not as a condiment or marinade.

CHEF'S NOTE: Low-sodium soy sauce may be substituted for the tamari.

NUTRITIONAL INFORMATION (1 TSP) 2 Calories, 0.0g Fat, 0.4g Carbohydrates, 0g Sugar, 0.1g Protein